Building State Capacity to Achieve Government Victory During Civil War

A Monograph
by
MAJ Christopher A. Ingels
United States Army

School of Advanced Military Studies
United States Army Command and General Staff College
Fort Leavenworth, Kansas

AY 2011

Approved for Public Release; Distribution is Unlimited

SCHOOL OF ADVANCED MILITARY STUDIES

MONOGRAPH APPROVAL

Major Christopher A. Ingels

Title of Monograph: Building State Capacity to Achieve Government Victory During Civil War

Approved by:

_____ Michael Mihalka, Ph.D.	Monograph Director
_____ John A. Kelly, COL, FA	Monograph Reader
_____ Thomas C. Graves, COL, IN	Director, School of Advanced Military Studies
_____ Robert F. Baumann, Ph.D.	Director, Graduate Degree Programs

Disclaimer: Opinions, conclusions, and recommendations expressed or implied within are solely those of the author, and do not represent the views of the US Army School of Advanced Military Studies, the US Army Command and General Staff College, the United States Army, the Department of Defense, or any other US government agency. Cleared for public release: distribution unlimited.

Abstract

BUILDING STATE CAPACITY TO ACHIEVE GOVERNMENT VICTORY DURING CIVIL WAR by Major Christopher A. Ingels, U.S. Army, 69 pages

Focusing efforts toward building security force capability without increasing state capacity is an ineffective strategy to achieve government victory in civil war. The purpose of this monograph is to advance and test the hypothesis that simultaneously building state capacity while expanding military capability is a more effective strategy for achieving government victory when conducting civil war. Developing state capacity to sustain Security Sector Reform (SSR) is also important to the current United States' strategy for increasing the likelihood of an Afghan governmental victory over Taliban rebels in Operation Enduring Freedom.

Current United States' Army doctrine--Field Manual (FM) 3-07, *Stability Operations,* and FM 3-24, *Counterinsurgency Operations*--attempts to address both state capacity and security force development by providing useful methods for combating insurgency while also addressing all aspects of state capacity building. However, flaws in this doctrine steer leaders toward focusing resources on troubled regions of conflict, thereby ignoring peaceful areas under government control. Since conflicted regions lack continuous peace, efforts to implement a stability strategy amount to little more than humanitarian relief, and fail to add capacity that strengthen a state's ability to achieve victory, and maintain peace once the war's outcome is determined.

This monograph finds that a simultaneous effort to combat rebels, and provide humanitarian relief in conflict zones, while building state capacity in peaceful regions, is a more effective strategy for achieving government victory in civil war. Additionally, only when a state strengthens its institutions leading to a prosperous economy, is it able to move beyond self-sufficiency and stand a greater chance of achieving victory in civil war. To determine how simultaneously building state capacity and security force capability increases the likelihood of government victory in civil war, this monograph uses a qualitative case study analysis method of difference approach to compare subject characteristics that result in two different outcomes--government victory and government defeat. The two selected case studies--Colombia and South Vietnam--represent similar hybrid and compound war characteristics similar to the current conflict occurring in Afghanistan.

The Colombia and South Vietnam case studies demonstrate how dynamic interaction between variables of state capacity, a nation's situational environment, and political leadership decisions, work to create strong state capability leading to government victory in civil war (Colombia), or adversely affected capacity's components resulting in weak capability and vulnerability (South Vietnam). Similar to Colombia's experience, Afghanistan's government has the possibility of attaining victory over Taliban rebels if foreign development aid shifts toward improving societal conditions and industry in peaceful regions of the country under government control. Simultaneously continuing humanitarian assistance and denying key areas to insurgent forces in the South will slowly increase the Afghan governments' ability to sustain a larger security force and provide responsive civil service institutions.

TABLE OF CONTENTS

ILLUSTRATIONS

Page

Introduction

Security progress . . . is the foundation for everything else, for the governance progress, the economic progress, rule-of-law progress, and so forth. Obviously, they influence security as well. They can either reinforce it or they can undermine it. And the . . . trick is to get all of it moving so that you're spiraling upward where one initiative reinforces another.

— General David H. Petraeus, *Meet the Press*, August 15, 2010

Focusing efforts toward building security force capability without increasing state capacity is an ineffective strategy to achieve government victory in civil war. The purpose of this monograph is to advance and test the hypothesis that simultaneously building state capacity while expanding military capability is a more effective strategy for achieving government victory while conducting civil war. Developing state capacity to sustain Security Sector Reform (SSR) is also important to the current United States' strategy for increasing the likelihood of an Afghan governmental victory over Taliban rebels in Operation Enduring Freedom.

In "The Dynamics of Civil War Duration and Outcome," Karl R. de Rouen and David Sobek claim there are four end states to civil war--government victory, rebel victory, truce, or treaty--that are largely determined by a state's bureaucratic capability, as opposed to a focused military effort.[1] In contrast, *Securing the Peace, the Durable Settlement of Civil Wars*, Monica Toft finds civil wars ending with a clear military victor as most important for gaining a binding peace. Toft argues that undergoing SSR is critical for creating a strong apparatus to ensure post civil war unity.[2] Thus, military action is necessary for gaining a one-sided victory.

However, the durability of peace depends on a state's capacity for implementing that peace and managing SSR. A weak state capability will most likely result in a weak security force,

---

[1]Karl R.de Rouen, and David Sobek, "The Dynamics of Civil War Duration and Outcome," *Journal of Peace Research* (2004): 303.

[2]Monica Duffy Toft, *Securing the Peace, The Durable Settlement of Civil Wars* (Princeton: Princeton University Press, 2010), 2, 12-13, 37-38.

thereby increasing the chances of renewed conflict or rebel victory. Unfortunately, de Rouen, Sobek, and Toft, focus on civil wars' outcome as attained and maintained by using only one aspect of state capacity. This fails to show how a state constructs capability to reach victory as a civil war outcome, or sustain SSR once the outcome is determined.

Current United States' Army doctrine--Field Manual (FM) 3-07, *Stability Operations,* and FM 3-24, *Counterinsurgency Operations*--attempts to address both state capacity development and security force capability by providing useful methods for combating insurgency while also addressing all aspects of state capacity building. However, flaws in this doctrine steer leaders toward focusing resources on troubled regions of conflict, thereby ignoring peaceful areas under government control.[3] Since conflicted regions lack continuous peace, efforts to implement FM 3-07's five-part stability strategy amount to little more than humanitarian relief, and fail to add capacity that will strengthen the state's ability to achieve victory and maintain peace once the war's outcome is determined.[4]

To promote further debate on state capacity and government victory during civil war, and its implications for U.S. Army doctrine, this monograph finds that a simultaneous effort to combat rebels, and provide humanitarian relief in conflict zones, while building state capacity in peaceful regions, is a more effective strategy for achieving government victory in civil war. Additionally, this monograph finds that once a state strengthens institutions leading to a prosperous economy, can it begin to move beyond self-sufficiency, thus standing a greater chance of achieving victory.

---

[3]U.S. Army, Field Manual (FM) 3-24, *Counterinsurgency Operations*, 2006 (Washington, DC: Government Printing Office, 2006), 5-1-5-5.

[4]U.S. Army, Field Manual (FM) 3-07, *Stability Operations*, 2008 (Washington, DC: Government Printing Office, 2008), IV, 1-4, 1-8, 1-16 - 1-18, 2-4 - 2-5.

To make this case, this monograph will explain and test its hypothesis in four parts: literature review, methodology, qualitative case study analysis, and finally, a closing analysis with recommendations for adjusting U.S. Army doctrine to build effective state capacity. The literature review section will critically survey current literature on capacity development to discover a working definition of "state capacity," identify its component variables, and describe how various components interact to generate--or dismantle--state capacity. This section will also review current U.S. Army doctrine and discuss how doctrine reflects various thoughts on building state capacity.

The monograph's second part, methodology, explains the choice of using a qualitative case study analysis to differentiate between two outcomes--government victory and rebel victory--for testing the hypothesis that both state capacity and security force development are necessary to defeat an insurgency. The methodology also explains why selecting conflicts in Colombia and South Vietnam serve as extreme examples for analysis over other civil war cases when compared to current activities taking place in Afghanistan. Such conflicts must possess characteristics of hybrid war, compound war, or both, to represent attributes of the current conflict in Afghanistan.

Frank G. Hoffman in "Hybrid vs. Compound War" defines hybrid war as an enemy simultaneously and adaptively employing a combination of conventional weapons, irregular tactics, terrorism, and criminal behavior, to obtain political objectives. Compound war is the simultaneous use of regular conventional forces with dispersed irregular forces.[5] Finally, the methodology section will provide measurement criteria for determining if a state is poised to achieve successfully victory during civil war, or is trending toward defeat.

The third section, case study analysis of Colombia and South Vietnam, will use the literature review's state capacity model and definitions as measured according to processes within

---

[5]Frank G. Hoffman, "Hybrid vs. Compound War," *Armed Forces Journal*, (October 2009): 1.

the methodology section, for differentiating between how building state capacity and security force capability lead to government victory or defeat in civil war. These case studies will also demonstrate the criticality of where capacity development takes place, and what aspects of capacity become developed, as necessary for successfully strengthening a nations' capacity for achieving victory.

Lastly, the fourth part of this monograph will end by comparing state capacity and security force case study outcomes to current activities taking place in Afghanistan, implemented by using current Army doctrine. Recommendations will follow the analysis to suggest doctrine revisions for better implementing methods that build state capacity and security force capability for achieving government victory during civil war.

Literature Review

The literature review section consists of two parts: it first surveys current academic literature to identify prevailing thoughts explaining state capacity, then reviews U.S. Army doctrine to determine if the doctrines' methods advance or detract from building state capacity. The academic review informs this monograph of various positions and theories, which define state capacity, explain its variables, describe variable interactions, and provide methods for measuring capacity's growth or decline. The monograph uses this literature to form a working definition of "state capacity," identify its component variables, and describe how variable interaction creates or dismantles state capacity, to apply against two case studies that explain how building state capacity and security force capability lead to government victory, or defeat, in civil war. Review of U.S. Army doctrine demonstrates how doctrines' capacity building methods address all variables of state capacity, but contains flaws that inadvertently harm development and weaken a government's ability to achieve victory during civil war.

There exists a vast literature discussing different definitions of what state capacity consists of, how it forms, how it functions, and what purpose state capacity holds for a nations' development and defense. A critical problem within this literature is the lack of a single overarching definition and model connecting the literatures' various thoughts, thereby falling short of explaining how a nation may harness the aspects of capacity to build a stronger state. Mauricio Cardenas, Marcela Eslava, and Santiago Ramirez, in "External Wars, Internal Conflict and State Capacity: Panel Date Evidence," finds the state capacity discussion takes place between the aspects of military capability, bureaucratic and administrative ability, and the legal-fiscal context of economic capacity.[6] Karl de Rouen and David Sobek, in "Dynamics of Civil War Duration and Outcome," emphasize the importance of Democratic government and bureaucratic institutions as necessary capacities for a state victory in civil war. These authors find a closed autocratic government, with a strong military, may increase a populations' "grievance" against the state thereby leading to greater rebel support and a prolonged conflict.[7]

Timothy Besley, in an interview with "Voxtalks," also recognizes the importance of states' having an inclusive governing system as necessary to foster national development. Besley refers to 'cohesive institutions' as the dynamic of "citizen control" over methods a state uses to tax and spend resources. Besley therefore defines state capacity as the ability of a government to respond "to those demand-side factors" that are the nature of political institutions.[8] Besley next takes the aspects of governing and bureaucratic capacities and links them to economics with Persson Torsten in "State Capacity, Conflict and Development," where the authors advance a

---

[6]Mauricio Cardenas, Marcela Eslava, and Santiago Ramirez, "External Wars, Internal Conflict and State Capacity: Panel Date Evidence," *Latin America Initiative* (2010): 2.

[7]de Rouen and Sobek, 305-308.

[8]Timothy Besley interview by Romesh Vaitilingam, in "State Capacity and Development," *Vox Talks* (June 2011), 2.

theory that growth in state capacity forms around a complimentary relationship between the fiscal and legal abilities of a nation.[9] Thus, Besley finds state capacity as "those things the state invests in to become an effective organization," relying on the states' capability to tax, and its "legal capacity" to enforce property rights and regulate a market economy.[10]

Cardenas is also interested in economics as an aspect of state capacity when studying relationship differences that external and internal wars have on developing capacity. Cardenas first reviews the works of Charles Tilly who finds that nations tend to develop strong state capability when fighting external wars, because these wars have a unifying nature within a country that enables the state to form inclusive governance and efficiently harness national resources for its defense.[11] Cardenas then sites the work of Miguel Angel Centeno and Fernando Lopez-Alves who discover "potentially opposing effects" that external and internal wars have on developing state capacity. Where external wars tend toward unifying and spurring capacity building investments, internal wars are divisive and destructive, thereby leading to less economic investment resulting in a weakened state capability.[12]

Important to this monograph is that Cardenas, Eslava, and Ramirez, review various aspects of state capacity--military, governance, bureaucracy, and economics--and compare the differences in development between states fighting external and internal conflicts--like Colombia and South Vietnam. In "Under-Investment in State Capacity: The Role of Inequality and Political Instability," Mauricio Cardenas and Didem Tuzemen cite the importance that wealth, investments, and tax collection have on determining state self-sufficiency. This contribution

---

[9]Timothy Besley and Persson Torsten, "State Capacity, Conflict and Development," (Monograph, St. Louis: Econometric Society 2008), 2-3.

[10]Besley interview by Romesh Vaitilingam, 1.

[11]Cardenas, Eslava, and Ramirez, 2-3.

[12]Ibid., 3, 25-26.

assists in explaining differences between humanitarian relief and development assistance that increases a states' capacity. Conversely, in *Making Democracy Work: Civic Traditions in Modern Italy*, Robert Putnam finds that economics and governance is not the central cause building strong state capacity. Instead, economic and government institutions rely on interactions within a populations' civic culture that create "trust, norms, and networks" which make possible society's functioning as a whole, especially "secondary organizations" since he finds they "represent historical" relationships among equal groups which differ from the hierarchical nature of political parties.[13]

Putnam's observations regarding the historical development of civil society and its impact on developing state capacity move this monograph to use a historical approach in studying state capacity development in Colombia and South Vietnam. Testing to discover if the people within these countries have a historical predisposition toward developing a stylized form of governance and capacity traditions, will assist in evaluating effects society has on development in conjunction with governance, bureaucracy, military capability, law, and economics. Matthew A. Kocher in "State Capacity as a Conceptual Variable" adds to the other works by identifying characteristics of strong and weak states, helping to gauge state viability in relation to levels of violence, rule of law, and prosperity.

This monograph is concerned with discovering how to build state capacity for better achieving government victory during civil war. This literature review has explained various ideas regarding state capacity that are helpful for understanding the different aspects, which develop a nations' capacity. However, there remains no overarching definition, or model to explain comprehensively how state capacity develops and functions. Mette Kjaer, Ole Hersted Hansen,

---

[13]Fienberg, Howard, review of *Making Democracy Work*, by Robert Putnam, *Howard Fienberg*, http://www.hfienberg.com/irtheory/putnam.html (accessed August 8, 2011), 1-2.

and Jens Peter Frolund Thomsen, in "Conceptualizing State Capacity," work to solve this problem by advancing a model that captures all aspects of state capacity as they interact in response to policy decisions. "Conceptualizing State Capacity" defines "state capacity," illustrates its variables, and demonstrates how those variables form capacity using a model that incorporates the military, social, political, bureaucratic, legal, and economic aspects, of state capacity found within this literature review.

This monograph will use the definition, variables, and model, advanced within "Conceptualizing State Capacity," augmented by findings in other works cited within this literature review, to define "state capacity," identify its components, and demonstrate how component interaction generates--or dismantles--state capacity. By defining state capacity, listing, and demonstrating linkages between variables, this monograph will show why combating rebellion and building state capacity simultaneously, increases a government's ability to achieve victory over insurgents during civil war.

Defining the State and State Capacity

In "State Capacity as a Conceptual Variable," Matthew Kocher notes the common function of a state is its ability to "monopolize the means of organized physical violence" within set territorial boundaries. When states are unable to dominate, groups within the state find a need to provide security themselves, creating an environment for violence or civil war to emerge between formerly "non-mobilized" entities.[14] Monica Toft in *Securing the Peace* defines civil war as a fight between two or more organized combatants able to harm one another within the borders of a recognized state.[15] To Kocher, these definitions fail to explain how a country loses

---

[14]Matthew A. Kocher, "State Capacity as a Conceptual Variable," *Yale Journal of International Affairs* (2010): 138.

[15]Toft, 9-10.

control because most observers only focus on security aspects of state authority, while neglecting

other factors that comprise a states' ability to control differing groups within its borders.[16]

Defining "state capacity" and its various components, in relation to a nation's formation, assist in

understanding how a government gains control (power) over its territory and people. By

understanding the attributes determining a sovereigns' control, can assist outside observers in

recognizing the various causes of government victory, or defeat, in preventing or ending civil

war. This section defines state capacity, lists its components, and then ends by illustrating how

linkages between variables determine a nation's ability to control.

Mette Kjaer, Ole Hansen, and Jens Thomsen in "Conceptualizing State Capacity," define

state capacity as the ability of a government to formulate and carryout policies. The purpose of

these polices--whether to advance economic, social, or security aims--depend on political

leadership, rule of law, and society.[17] Most nation-states form these components through the

"interface of war and capitalist development," where conflict made it necessary to increase

domestic resources through better organization by enlarging public and private administration.[18]

States having limited social and economic influence gradually expanded to gain greater

surveillance ability and promote industrial development for generating wealth necessary to

conduct war. Growth required former despotic rulers to negotiate and share decision-making

powers with other "civil groups" and organizations, thereby tying society's influence to

government's functioning. As elites gradually transitioned power by co-opting larger segments of

---

[16] Kocher, 139-140.

[17] Mette Kjaer, Ole H. Hansen, and Jens P. Frolund Thomsen, "Conceptualizing State Capacity," *Democracy, the State, and Administrative Reforms Research Report* No. 6 (April 2002): 17-18, 20.

[18] Ibid., 9.

society, the state created "infrastructure power"--the ability to implement political decisions throughout civil-society using rule-based institutions.[19]

The transition between "despotic power" and "infrastructure power" becomes the first area to observe when investigating state capacity--has a state moved from controlling its territory by one ruling class, to one controlled by incorporating broader society? Expanding participation to different groups allows a nation to harness greater resources to expand its capability. This is an argument supported in works earlier cited by de Rouen, Sobek, and Besley. Expanding participation requires creating rules to make fair how actors participate in decision-making, form institutions, and implement approved policies. These rules are the foundation for an impartial justice system and an interest based political system (institutions) needed to manage the enlargement of state affairs.[20] Thus, state actors, governing bureaucracy, and society, create the foundation for state capacity--the ability of states to design and carryout policies.[21]

This approach also demonstrates how states adjust by interacting within their environment. State capacity depends on society's capability, bureaucratic structures, and outside influences. How government is able to shift policies moving the nation toward a new direction is constrained by environmental factors. Generating capacity requires an open system with interaction between political leaders, society, and other independent states.[22]

In summary, state capacity initially consisted of "despotic power" where a single elite and its administration controlled nations' people and territory. However, outside competition and the threat of war with other states created a need to generate more resources for conquest or protection, forcing elites to share power with a broader public. This created new processes and

---

[19]Ibid.

[20]Ibid., 9-10, 17-18.

[21]Ibid., 20.

[22]Ibid., 10.

institutions to govern policy-making, implement approved policies, expand economic growth, and manage internal and external affairs affecting the state, called "infrastructure power."

State capacity to control its territory now depends on the ability of political leaders, governing bureaucracy, and the overall public, to sustain itself in an open world system that requires making changes based-on its internal and external situation. Having identified emerging components of state capacity--used to manage its environment through infrastructure power-- how does one categorize components to better distinguish their variables and track linkages necessary for harnessing capacity?

Components of State Capacity

There are three components forming state capacity: central capacities, enhancing mechanisms, and enabling societal conditions (see figure 1). "Central capacities" are traits beneficial to states--wealth creation, bureaucratic organization, specialized administration, treasury control of public finances, and an externally oriented military.[23]

"Capacity enhancing mechanisms" are actions that political leaders take that may help or hinder the central capacities. These actions include designing standard laws for solving business conflict, empowering local leaders to deliver services, create a responsive public sector, and establishing relationships with outside entities, states, and institutions.[24] The enabling factors of state capacity depend on societal conditions--like education, health, and industry--and determine how the central capacities will perform since organizations are resourced using the nations' population. Therefore, a government that builds popular trust, an expanding private sector, educational opportunities, civic organization, prepares against outside threats, and tends to the

---

[23]Ibid., 21-22.

[24]Ibid., 22-24.

nations' position within the world market place, is using core capacity to enable society for improving mechanisms used in adjusting to the world environment. This functioning dynamic enhances state capacity.[25]

Central capacities	Capacity enhancing mechanisms	Capacity enabling factors
Fiscal revenue creation Principles of bureaucratic organization Specialized and differentiated administrative system Strong Treasury control of public finances (internal state control Outward oriented military defense (national autonomy	Close ties or corporatist arrangements (conflict solving capacity) i.e. institutionalized bargaining, types of governance of the market system Empowered local authorities (delivery of services) Flexible public sector Leadership, role of politicians (governance) Types of ties with external actors and institutions	Governance generating legitimacy, trust and reciprocity Growing private sector, internal organization High levels of education Level of societal organization External threats to the state Position in the international division of labor

Figure 1. State Capacities

Source: Mette Kjaer, Ole H. Hansen, and Jens P. Frolund Thomsen, "Conceptualizing State Capacity," *Democracy, the State, and Administrative Reforms Research Report* No. 6 (April 2002): 22.

Military force and wealth creation are two additional variables needed for composing state capacity. Military force is the tool used for removing internal and external threats to state authority. Wealth creation and taxation are conditional variables that highlight the state's ability to mobilize resources, serving as a "bottom-line" indicator of state capacity. Countries must have

---

[25]Ibid.

12

a "tax-generating" ability to pay expenses for its organizations' workforce, and provide resources to carryout policies.[26]

Mauricio Cardenas and Didem Tuzemen in "Under-Investment in State Capacity: The Role of Inequality and Political Instability," detail the importance of wealth creation and taxation by narrowly defining state capacity as the power to raise tax revenue. States unable to collect taxes are limited in the number of services they can provide for bettering society and protecting the state from outside entities.[27] Their research finds states that fight external wars have greater political stability, inclusive political institutions, and larger capacity, because they effectively move resources toward the nation's defense. However, civil wars are "a measure of political instability" that negatively affect wealth, and result in less investment to state capacity, because they are highly destructive.[28]

Civil war reflects political instability between groups that want to breakaway or dominate the nation's core capacity. Rebels seek to achieve this by disrupting society and governing mechanisms thereby destroying wealth. As a state loses resources, its policy choices (ability) become constrained in dealing with the war. Therefore, a government must adopt a strategy to combat rebels while simultaneously building capacity in peaceful areas it controls to maintain wealth creation. Peaceful areas working under the rule of law encourage investment that creates wealth. How do the variable interactions of wealth creation, military force, central capacity, enhancing mechanisms, and enabling social conditions, determine if a state is generating weak or strong capacity?

---

[26]Ibid., 21, 23.

[27]Mauricio Cardenas and Didem Tuzemen, "Under-Investment in State Capacity: The Role of Inequality and Political Instability," *Global Economy and Development* (September 2010): 2.

[28]Ibid., 2-5.

Dynamics of Variable Interaction on State Capacity

State capacity provides government the ability to formulate and carryout policies for addressing challenges in the world environment.[29] This capacity also determines the span of control a state has over the population within its borders.[30] How much capacity a state is able to produce through the interactions of central capacity, enhancing mechanisms, and enabling societal conditions, depend on the relationship between political leaders and society.

Kjaer, Hansen, and Thomsen developed a model—"Capacity as a Dynamic Relationship Model" (figure 2)--illustrating how leadership decisions and popular support cause the three categories to interact, thereby forming capacity. If a state's goal is to create a strong centralized capacity for control, or a weaker decentralized capacity, depends on the character and preferences of government leaders and the population. Nation's where leaders (political regime) are supported by a majority of the population usually have stronger state capacity because government policies are accepted, thereby moving efficiently through the rules process (enhancing mechanism), then willfully enacted through core capacity institutions (capacity). States with weak leadership, or vastly unpopular leaders, undergo friction in devising new plans and having them carried-out through its central capacities. Interest groups and society can use the rule system and bureaucracy to push back, or impede, unpopular plans.[31]

Therefore, relationships between leaders and society drive the dynamic interactions between capacity variables that form the basis for strong or weak states. Political leaders can also increase capacity by enacting plans that improve societal conditions and enhancing mechanisms. Requiring universal education, proscribing business incentives, facilitating interaction with

---

[29]Kjaer, Hansen, and Thomsen, 9-10.

[30]Kocher, 138.

[31]Kjaer, Hansen, and Thomsen, 22-25.

outside entities, or reforming the legal code, are policy examples that may improve society's condition and capacity-enhancing mechanisms. These improvements expand society's capability, further strengthening institutional ability, which influence increasing wealth creation--"the bottom-line" indicator of state capacity.[32]

Wealth provides resources to meet leaderships' policy goals. A nation's wealth is important for determining which demands a state can action. Poor countries are less able to improve societal conditions or enhancing mechanisms that generate capacity for reinvestment toward future returns, because they lack resources (wealth) to invest in civic-institutions. A lack of resources represent weak state capacity because it "prevents" leaders from "actively initiating change" to deal with problems. Wealthy States have resources making them capable of adjusting the course of societal development in response to a changing environment, while meeting current operational demands.[33]

Building strong state capacity allows a country's leadership and citizenry the ability to adjust to new environmental challenges by changing policies affecting societal conditions and mechanisms that form central capacity. This requires aligning support between political leadership and popular will and depends on a states' ability to foster wealth creation. Lacking resources constrains the governments' flexibility to respond to environmental threats--like expanding its army to defeat an insurgency or hostile neighbor.

Leaders can grow wealth through plans that invest resources in societal development and improve regulatory guidelines. Improving these two categories seamlessly fosters states' central capacity organizations, resulting in a wider and more competent ability to manage the environment. There are five characteristics signifying weak and strong state capacity.

---

[32]Ibid., 21-25.

[33]Ibid., 21.

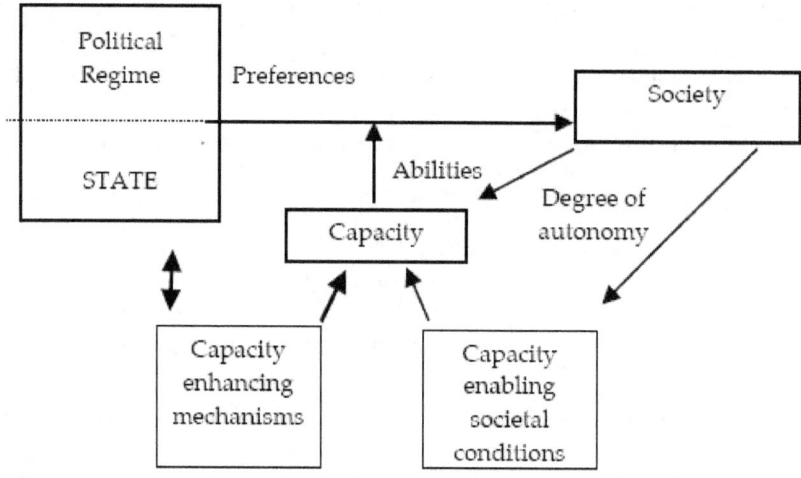

Figure 2. Capacity as a Dynamic Relationship
Source: Mette Kjaer, Ole H. Hansen, and Jens P. Frolund Thomsen, "Conceptualizing State Capacity," *Democracy, the State, and Administrative Reforms Research Report* No. 6 (April 2002): 25.

Characteristics of Strong and Weak States

Matthew Kocher provides five characteristics identifying states as weak or strong helping to explain causes leading to civil war. First, territorial, and administrative centralization characterize strong states. Weak states tend to be decentralized with competing administrations or have territories physically separated. Decentralized entities usually create the "fault-line" for where separations in the state occur.[34]

Secondly, strong states have wealth or "fiscal capacity," allowing them to tax and borrow to meet planned objectives. Strong states are able to gather resources because they are physically available, or they are skilled at getting them. Weak states susceptible to civil war usually have

---

[34]Kocher, 141.

vast disparities in income amongst the population. Third, a professional and autonomous

bureaucracy (including the military) characterizes a strong state. Legal methods for selecting,

training, disciplining, and credentialing officials, while providing a salary, removes an officials'

loyalty from an elite or private interest to minimize corruption. Weak states have no bureaucratic

autonomy, where officials exploit positions for personal gain.[35]

Fourth, strong states allow leaders a degree of independence to create and implement

policies. Weak states occur when a large number of actors can veto policy execution, making it

overly difficult to accomplish an action.[36] However, if a government becomes too autonomous it

risks becoming corrupt, resulting in weak institutions.[37] Finally, Kocher finds strong states are

characterized by the "quantity and quality" of military assets, like troops, tanks, and aircraft.

Sizeable armies, or qualitative armies, are able to deter external attack by neighbors and

discourage domestic groups from attempting to overthrow or break away from the state.[38]

State capacity is the ability of a nation to formulate and carryout policies. It exercises this

power using despotic institutions of ruling elites, or by infrastructure power from an expansive

bureaucracy. The ruling power, bureaucratic institutions, and society--known as central capacity,

capacity enhancing mechanisms, and capacity enabling societal conditions--dynamically interact

to form a strong or weak state capability. A nation's ability to generate wealth is a key conditional

variable affecting its choices for building administration, changing strategies, and modifying

social development, to manage emerging national challenges. To review, the five variables

critical for developing state capacity are central capacities, capacity-enhancing mechanisms,

enabling societal conditions, military force, and wealth creation. Policy decisions made by

---

[35]Ibid., 41-142.

[36]Ibid., 142.

[37]Kjaer, Hansen, and Thomsen, 11-12.

[38]Kocher, 142-143.

governing leaders, and society's acceptance of government, drive these five variables to interact throughout civil society within the situational environment and determine if a state is strengthening or weakening its capacity to respond to events.

In "Measuring State Capacity: Theoretical and Empirical Implications for the Study of Civil Conflict," Cullen S. Hendrix finds the subject of state capacity lacks a "precise definition and measurement," as most concept ideas and uses stress military capacity, bureaucratic administrative capacity, and the quality of political institutions. Hendrix's article reviews nineteen state capacity theories and quantitatively tests each theory's validity using principal factor analysis of fifteen operational measures of capacity--like military expenditure per capita and bureaucratic quality--to discover if a common set of variables exist across the several theories. The purpose of Hendrix's study is to better define and measure state capacity's link to civil war causes.[39]

Factor analysis is a quantitative methodology that studies if dynamic relationships between a set of observable variables are better illustrated using a smaller set of underlying factors. Hendrix observes that the nineteen competing definitions and functions of state capacity suggest this concept is potentially "multidimensional." Factor analysis works to discover if multiple variables of the competing theorists overlap, creating a group of characteristics that can more usefully describe state capacity.[40]

Hendrix's study finds three common definitions of state capacity--economic development, bureaucratic capacity, and political institutional coherence--are all "collinear" and develop from internal structural causes. Therefore, deciding which variables to choose for testing

---

[39]Cullen S. Hendrix, "Measuring State Capacity: Theoretical and Empirical Implications for the Study of Civil Conflict," *Journal of Peace Research*, 2010: 273, 281, 283.

[40]Ibid., 280.

"must be made" on a theoretical basis using a multivariate approach to model more accurately state capacity. This research also finds variables of bureaucratic quality and total taxes/Gross Domestic Product (GDP), as correlative to most state capacity arguments and observed testing's.[41]

Cullen Hendrix's research becomes important to this monograph because his findings provide a useful methodology for measuring the five dynamic variables found within the "Conceptualizing State Capacity" model. Research findings also guide this monograph toward selecting case studies possessing rich data for observing bureaucratic quality and tax capacity per GDP, as these variables provide measures to "Conceptualizing State Capacity's" central capacity and wealth creation variables.

Building State Capacity and Implications for U.S. Army Doctrine

Current U.S. Army stability and counterinsurgency operations doctrine is implicitly linked to building state capacity, where the desired end state of each operation is to assist building a nation to such a point that its leaders and people are able to address their own problems effectively, otherwise the state will fail. Army doctrine reflects the various thoughts within the state capacity discussion as it has devised tasks for addressing all aspects of capacity building, like governance, rule of law, and economics. U.S. Army's Field Manual (FM) 3-07, *Stability Operations*, provides a framework for military and civilian leaders to conduct a "comprehensive approach" using all instruments of U.S. national power to "create an environment that fosters host-nation institutional development"--or capacity building. This manual provides a five-part strategy with accompanying tasks--safe and secure environment, rule of law, social well-being, stable governance, and sustainable economy--that link to the U.S. Department of State's post-

---

[41]Ibid., 273, 282-283.

conflict reconstruction responsibilities, which are necessary for setting security and rebuilding national self-sufficiency.[42]

Likewise, U.S. Army FM 3-24, *Counterinsurgency Operations*, provides a three-stage process to attain a stable and secure environment that allow stability operations (capacity building) to begin initial stage "stop the bleeding," middle stage "recovery," and late stage "movement to self-sufficiency." Leaders use FM 3-07s' five-part strategy during the late stage to implement tasks, thereby theoretically bringing a troubled country away from civil war violence toward peaceful self-sustainment.[43]

However, this doctrine has flaws because it inadvertently steers capacity development to take place within zones of conflict where divisiveness and destruction are greatest during civil war. Therefore, development fails to take place since civil war violence disrupts capacity's variable interactions and destroys wealth. Resources invested within conflict zones do not spur the private reinvestment required for expanding state capacity, thereby amounting to humanitarian relief--not capacity building development.

FM 3-24's, *Counterinsurgency Operations*, three stage process for conducting counterinsurgency operations (COIN), and its' clear-hold-build approach for implementing a COIN strategy, is similar to the Pacification/Strategic Hamlet program used during the Vietnam War. The South Vietnam case study demonstrates that Pacification required a large U.S. military force to clear Vietminh insurgents from South Vietnam, and was ineffective at developing South Vietnamese state capacity.[44]

---

[42]U.S. Army, Field Manual 3-07, IV, 1-4, 1-8, 1-16, 1-18, 2-4-2-5.

[43]U.S. Army, Field Manual 3-24, 5-1-5-5.

[44]Ibid., 5-1, 5-2 – 5-5.

Within FM 3-24's suggested three-phase campaign, the first stage is to seize the initiative from the insurgents, "protect the population," and set conditions for future activity where offensive operations are "complemented" by stability operations. The second stage seeks to achieve stability by having COIN forces implement logical lines of operation--like civil security, military force development, governance, essential services, and economic development--to strengthen host nation governmental legitimacy, and increase intelligence gathering. The final stage expands stability operations across "contested regions," where host nation forces assume a larger role against rebels and the government becomes capable of managing its country while further isolating the insurgency.[45]

FM 3-24 next advises a clear-hold-build approach for conducting COIN operations in areas "experiencing further overt insurgent operations,"[46] which is similar to the Pacification and "New Life Hamlet Strategy"[47] advocated in U.S. Army FM 100-1, Change-1, December 1960. According to Andrew J. Birtle in *U.S. Army Counterinsurgency and Contingency Operations Doctrine, 1942-1976*, FM 100-1, Change-1, calls for COIN forces to divide an Area of Operations into "subareas" that forces seal, scour, and pacify "before moving to the next . . . where government control gradually spread across the countryside like a drop of oil on water."[48]

Similarly, FM 3-24 explains' "the pattern of this approach is to clear, hold, and build one village, area, or city--and then reinforce success by expanding to other areas." Clear-hold-build's "primary tasks" are to provide continuous security for the population, remove the insurgent presence, reinforce political dominance, implement the rule of law, and rebuild host nation

[45]Ibid., 5-2 – 5-3.

[46]Ibid., 5-18.

[47]Graham A. Cosmas, *United States Army in Vietnam, MACV, The Joint Command in the Years of Escalation,* (Washington, D.C. United States Army Center of Military History 2006), 75-76, 139.

[48]Andrew J. Birtle, *U.S. Army Counterinsurgency and Contingency Operations Doctrine, 1942-1976,* (Washington, D.C.: United States Army Center of Military History, 2006), 168-170.

institutions. After clearing an area, "ideally" host nation forces will hold the newly secured territory. Once friendly forces control an area can operations move to the strategy's build phase where growing support for host nation government is sought by providing a combination of population security and humanitarian relief work to meet the populations "needs and expectations" through "economic, social, cultural, and medical" projects.[49]

A key weakness to the Pacification strategy--or clear-hold-build approach--is that it requires the host nation government and population to possess the resources and skills necessary to secure effectively, then administer, newly reclaimed territory in contested regions of civil war conflict. This strategy also relies on the assumption that people living within conflict zones will popularly support a governments' leadership, believing them legitimate for providing relief services and improving schools.[50] Finally, and most counter-productive, the strategy inadvertently directs a disproportionate amount of military and economic aid into contested zones, where outside resources stand little chance of spurring local investment due to the destructive nature of the conflict.[51]

Commanders who implement the Pacification/Clear-hold-build approach to COIN may find host nation security forces, and governing officials, unable to secure and administer the rule of law in newly cleared areas. This deficiency adversely affects the overall strategy by requiring additional coalition forces to administer cleared territory, creating a negative trend of drawing technical experts and development aid away from building within peaceful areas under government control into the conflict zones' cleared areas. Territory held by friendly forces does not necessarily make such territory uncontested, especially if home to a hostile populace

---

[49]U.S. Army, FM 3-24, 5-18 – 5-21.

[50]Ibid., 5-21.

[51]Cardenas and Tuzemen, 2-5.

supportive of the insurgency. Thus, conflict continues and no meaningful reinvestment will take place.

Because Pacification/Clear-hold-build directs a majority of resources into contested conflict zones, this approach fails to expand host nation capacity within peaceful regions already held by the government. Aid investments made to peaceful areas can benefit all aspects of state capacity because they promote predictable returns on reinvestment. Reinvestment generates greater human and financial resources for growing state capacity--as later demonstrated in the Colombia case study using the "Virtuous circle of security."[52]

Colonel Russell W. Volckmann, author of U.S. Army FM 31-20, *Operations Against Guerilla Forces, February 1951*, introduced the idea of dividing a theater of operations into "three zones"--areas controlled by insurgents, areas controlled by government, and areas contested between the two zones. Colonel Volckmann also recommended three objectives when conducting COIN--isolate insurgents from their popular support base, deny insurgents access to outside support, and finally, destroy the insurgents.[53] Using Colonel Volckmann's approach, leaders can formulate a strategy that simultaneously expands state capacity within peaceful regions under government control, while isolating insurgents in contested areas by sectioning a nation into three zones.

The Colombia case study will demonstrate that as a state builds its resource capacity by expanding and professionalizing its military-administrative capability, and fostering its economy for greater wealth creation, eventually makes the state self-sufficient by providing internal resources that strengthen its ability to interdict insurgent forces, gain control of contested regions,

---

[52]Republic of Colombia Ministry of National Defense, *Policy for the Consolidation of Democratic Security*, 17-18.

[53]Birtle, 135-137.

and strike into insurgent strongholds. Conducting offensive operations into insurgent territory allows a government to slowly diminish an insurgents' support capacity and remove links to its outside enablers. As an insurgents' capacity shrinks it becomes less effective.[54]

Territory reclaimed by the government does not automatically benefit the state until violence has decreased to a level where judicial administrators are able to enforce the rule of law without military assistance. Economic aid designated for reclaimed regions only serves as humanitarian relief designed to meet the immediate needs of the local population. Without a populations' willful observance to the rule of law, local investment in reclaimed regions risk being lost to renewed violence.[55]

Therefore, the state must already possess the capacity to generate needed resources in peaceful regions that can support future humanitarian efforts within reclaimed areas. As a state continues to grow a capacity to support its offensive momentum, while destroying rebel forces, an inclusive government positions the state for achieving a populations' acquiescence by allowing competing interests representation in government. Inclusive governance is one key method for attaining popular support and a willful observance to the rule of law.

Methodology

Quantitative and qualitative methodologies are two common approaches used by researchers to test and validate theoretical hypotheses. Quantitative research uses numerical data-- like surveys or database calculations--to test objectively a hypothesis under controlled conditions for observing statistical interactions that result in broad-based findings. These tests seek to

---

[54]Republic of Colombia Ministry of National Defense, 9-12, 16-17.

[55]Republic of Colombia National Planning Department and Department of Justice and Security, *Colombia's Strategy for Strengthening Democracy and Promoting Social Development*, (2007-2013), Final Version, (Columbian National Government, February 2007), 11-12.

observe relationships and differences between variables for discovering cause and effect, or other correlations between measured variables.[56]

Qualitative research uses non-numerical data, such as personal interviews, historical records, and participant observations, to form and validate new hypotheses from the information collected. This method looks at different sequence of events to find patterns or new ideas that result in detailed findings, or give multiple perspectives regarding a hypothesis' validity.[57] There are five qualitative research methods used to study and test a hypothesis: phenomenology, ethnography, case study research, grounded theory, and historical research. This monograph uses qualitative case study methodology because it provides' a detailed and wide-ranging account of one or more cases to discover and compare subject characteristics in relationship to the hypothesis.[58]

To determine how simultaneously building state capacity and security force capability increases the likelihood of government victory in civil war, this monograph uses the method of difference approach to compare case study characteristics that result in two different outcomes-- government victory and government defeat. The method of difference approach is a technique that compares cases with similar background characteristics, but different values on the study variable (state capacity), as a way to find new differences between the cases. Newly found differences can then serve as possible causes for the study variable (state capacity) or its possible effects--government victory or government defeat in civil war.[59]

---

[56]Burke Johnson and Larry Christensen, *Educational Research, Quantitative, Qualitative, and Mixed Approaches, Second Edition* (Boston: Pearson Education, Inc., 2004), 29-33.

[57]Ibid., 29-31, 45-48, 359-361.

[58]Ibid., 29-31, 363-379.

[59]Stephen Van Evera, *Guide to Methods for Students of Political Science*, (Ithaca: Cornell University Press, 1997), 11, 23, 57.

This monograph uses the literature review's "Conceptualizing State Capacity" definition, theoretical model, and capacity variables as the basis for observing affects that policy decisions have on the interaction of capacity variables, which form strong or weak state capacity. To review, central capacities, enhancing mechanisms, enabling societal conditions, military force, and wealth creation, are the five variables that comprise state capacity. It also uses historical information to observe and measure policy affects on state capacity variables for conducting qualitative analysis of differentiation using two civil wars (Colombia and South Vietnam), presenting two different outcomes--government victory and government defeat.[60]

To select cases for the method of difference approach, the *Correlates of War (COW) Projects' Intrastate War Data,* version 4.1, offers a range of four hundred and eleven civil war possibilities occurring between 1816 and 2010.[61] The purpose of this monograph is to offer future possibilities toward achieving an Afghanistan government victory over Taliban rebels. Thus, the monograph selects civil war case studies based on the criteria outlined below.

Conflicts must possess the characteristics of hybrid war, compound war, or both, to represent attributes similar to the current war in Afghanistan. This narrows the range of civil war possibilities to those occurring after World War II, and shortens the list to two hundred and thirty-three potential civil war cases. To refine further case study selections of remaining conflicts, this monograph reviews those civil wars which involve direct U.S. military advisory or operational support inside a conflicted nation that support government forces, thereby trimming the COW's database to a selection list of nineteen potential cases within fourteen countries identified below in figure 3.

---

[60]Ibid., 9-88.

[61]Meredith Reid Sarkees and Frank Wayman, *Resort to War: A Data Guide to Inter-State, Extra-State, Intra-State, and Non-State Wars, 1816-2007* (Washington, DC: CQ Press, 2010).

State Name	Start-End Dates	Outcome	Hybrid or Compound War
Afghanistan	2001-present	Ongoing	Both
Bosnia	1995	Government victory	Both
Cambodia	1971-1973	Government defeat	Compound
Colombia	1989-present	Trending government victory	Hybrid
Dominican Republic	1965	Continues below war level	Neither
El Salvador	1979-1992	Compromise	Neither
Guatemala	1966-1968	Government victory	Neither
Yugoslavia (Kosovo)	1998-1999	Government defeat	Hybrid
Laos	1964-1968	Government defeat	Compound
Lebanon	1958 1983-1984	Government victory Government defeat	Neither Both
Pakistan Waziristan	2004-2006	Government defeat	Hybrid
Philippines	1950 1972-1981 1972-1992 2000-2001, 2003, 2005-2006	Government victory Government victory Stalemate Continues below war level	Neither Neither Neither Hybrid
Somalia	1992-1994 2007	Compromise Government victory	Hybrid Hybrid
South Vietnam	1961-1973	Government defeat	Both

Figure 3. Post World War II Civil Wars with U.S. Involvement
Source: Meredith Reid Sarkees and Frank Wayman, *Resort to War: A Data Guide to Inter-State, Extra-State, Intra-State, and Non-State Wars, 1816-2007* (Washington, DC: CQ Press, 2010).

This list assists in choosing one case resulting in government victory--Colombia--and one case resulting in government defeat--South Vietnam--with characteristics similar to current state capacity and security building efforts occurring in Afghanistan. Colombia represents a case within the COW of trending government success at fighting an on-going hybrid style civil war, while slowly building state and security force capacity with U.S. assistance. These characteristics are similar to the COW's on-going, extra-state, war classification given to the current conflict in Afghanistan.[62]

South Vietnam represents a case study in government failure at fighting a prolonged compound civil war, with hybrid war characteristics, while receiving massive U.S. economic and military aid. This second case study assesses U.S. and South Vietnamese state building efforts in South Vietnam to determine how that nation's capacity was destroyed resulting in a North Vietnamese and Vietminh insurgent victory. Reasons for excluding the remaining eleven civil war cases as subjects for this study follow below.

The Dominican Republic,[63] El Salvador, Guatemalan,[64] and Philippine[65] civil wars do not meet this monograph's hybrid-compound war criteria since the nature of these conflicts resemble either conventional or traditional guerrilla style warfare. The current hybrid insurgency occurring within the Philippines between government forces, the Moro Islamic Liberation Front, and Abu Sayyaf remains confined to the Mindanao Island, which rarely affects the larger Philippine nation.[66] This insurgency's activity falls below the COW's criteria for war, and therefore does not make a suitable case study for this monograph.

---

[62]Ibid.

[63]Michael J. Kryzanek, *Latin American Politics and Development*, ed. Howard J. Wiarda and Harvey F. Kline (Boulder: Westview Press, 1990), 539-540.

[64]Kristan Skrede Gleditsch and Kyle Beardsley, "Nosy Neighbors, Third-Party Actors in Central American Conflicts," *Journal of Conflict Resolution* (June 2004): 386-387, 393, 399.

[65]Ernesto C. Torres, "A Success Story of Philippine Counterinsurgency: A Study of Bohol" (Master's thesis, Command and General Staff College, 2011), 1-3.

[66]Ibid., 12-13.

Civil wars in Cambodia[67] and Laos[68] illustrate two cases of prolonged compound warfare where both government and rebel forces received external military assistance. However, events in South Vietnam overshadowed neighboring conflicts in Cambodia and Laos due to the amount of U.S. support given toward preventing a communist takeover of the south. Thus, the larger conflict in South Vietnam provides a better selection of data for case study analysis.[69]

Bosnia[70] and Kosovo were not selected for research because their outcomes and subsequent peace enforcement was secured by the actions of the North Atlantic Treaty Organization and larger international community.[71] Somalia resembles Bosnia and Kosovo in that the international community forged, and continues to support, settlements made between conflicting clans that has enabled the formation of the Somali Transitional Federal Government (TFG).[72] The TFG has relied on international forces to prevent the al-Shabaab insurgency from gaining control of Mogadishu and southern Somalia.[73] Therefore, Somalia currently lacks sufficient data on state capacity and security force building to provide lessons for current capacity building operations in Afghanistan.

The Lebanese civil wars also serve as a poor example for determining how building state capacity increases the likelihood government victory during an internal conflict. Lebanon's

---

[67]Michael Radu, *The New Insurgencies, Anticommunist Guerrillas in the Third World* (New Brunswick: Transaction Publishers, 1990), 199-201.

[68]Xiaoming Zhang, "China's Involvement in Laos During the Vietnam War, 1963-1975," *Journal of Military History* (October 2002): 1142-1145, 1153, 1162.

[69]Ibid., 1160.

[70]Francesco Strazzari, *Shadow Globalization, Ethnic Conflicts and New Wars, A Political Economy of Intra-state War*, ed. Dietrich Jung (London: Routledge, 2003), 141-142.

[71]Tom Gallagher, *The Balkans in the New Millennium* (London: Routledge, 2005), 56, 60-63, 72-73, 132-133, 148.

[72]Walter S. Poole, *The Effort to Save Somalia* (Washington, DC: U.S. Government Printing Office, 2005), 1-2, 4-6.

[73]US Department of State, *Somalia.* September 26, 2011, http://www.state.gov/r/pa/ ei/bgn/2863 htm (accessed September 29, 2011), 1, 6.

hybrid civil war occurred due to its society's forming "militarized" self-governing enclaves, along sectarian lines, that fought to maintain regional control where no one groups was able to dominate the country. This civil war compounded when Palestinian refugees, Syria, Iran, and Israel, used Lebanon as a battleground for carrying out cross-border incursions, occupying territory, or implementing proxy wars to advance their security interests.[74] These factors make Lebanon a better subject for analyzing the formation, structure, and survival of non-state actors within the context of hybrid civil war.

The last potential case study for consideration is Pakistan's military campaign to defeat Taliban and al-Qaeda militants within its Waziristan Province. This conflict remains an inadequate choice because of the regions' significance as an insurgent base of support to the ongoing conflict in Afghanistan. Regular cross-border activity prevents Pakistan from standing alone as a distinct case study, instead making it an added factor when attempting to solve Afghanistan's civil war, thereby disqualifying this conflict for case study selection.[75]

Finally, this monograph will use Cullen S. Hendrix's suggested multivariate approach, with added focus on bureaucratic quality and tax capacity, as the method for measuring variables within the two case studies.[76] Detailed findings from the case studies will allow this monograph to propose new possibilities for achieving an Afghan government victory over Taliban rebels in civil war. This now brings the monograph to its third section--case study analysis--for testing the hypothesis using a qualitative case study methodology of differentiation to discover new variables explaining the outcomes of government victory and government defeat during civil war.

---

[74]Jurgen Endres, *Shadow Globalization, Ethnic Conflicts and New Wars, A Political Economy of Intra-state War*, ed. Dietrich Jung (London: Routledge, 2003), 122-128.

[75]Adeel Khan, "Pakistan in 2006, Safe Center, Dangerous Peripheries" *Asian Survey*, (January/February 2007), 127-128.

[76]Cullen S. Hendrix, "Measuring State Capacity: Theoretical and Empirical Implications for the Study of Civil Conflict" *Journal of Peace Research*, (2010): 273, 282-283.

Case Study I: State Capacity and Government Victory in Colombia

The third section of this monograph, case study analysis, uses the literature review's state capacity model and definitions to conduct an analysis of internal conflict within Colombia and South Vietnam to differentiate between how building state capacity and security force capability lead to government victory or defeat in civil war. Each case study uses a historical approach to discover how capacity variables formed within each nation's context and how government and U.S. support activities fostered or undermined capacity development during each country's civil war. Outcomes from these case studies will demonstrate the criticality of carefully determining where capacity development takes place and what aspects of capacity become developed to provide recommendations in the monographs' analysis and conclusion section for adjusting U.S. Army stability and counterinsurgency doctrine.

This first study compares state capacity variables to activities implemented by Colombia's government that led to victory over numerous insurgent groups since 2002. Harvey F. Kline's *State Building and Conflict Resolution in Colombia, 1986-1994*, provides historical detail of Colombia's capacity development from the country's inception as a Spanish colony into the current era. However, Kline fails to detail Colombia's crucial civil war--*La Violencia*--occurring between 1948 and 1965, which is critical for illustrating the link between rule of law development and stable governance. James L. Zackrison's "La Violencia in Colombia: An Anomaly in Terrorism," fills this gap, and explains the rise of modern insurgency in Colombia over the past fifty years.

Two important strategies formulated by the Colombian government--The Policy for the Consolidation of Democratic Security, and Colombia's Strategy for Strengthening Democracy and Promoting Social Development (2007-2013)--demonstrate the differences between conducting counterinsurgency-humanitarian relief operations, and developmental reconstruction that grow state capacity. Using this literature allows the monograph to demonstrate how interacting components of state capacity formed an increasingly stronger state measured by decreases in violence, reimplementation of law, and vast increases in prosperity. The Colombian case study demonstrates how simultaneous counterinsurgency and state-building operations-- conducted in peaceful regions under government control--can lead to government victory in civil war.

Through its early history, Colombia held a weak state capacity due to its decentralized governing authority, lack of professional bureaucracy, and partisan based rule of law that gave the country a weak ability for controlling its territory and citizen's behavior. Ironically, Colombia is a country that held all prerequisites for formulating strong state capacity--inclusive government, free-market institutions, and a resourceful society. It possessed wealth from a prosperous economy and maintained a standing army, both important variables for creating strong state capacity.[77]

The Colombian case study demonstrates how states do not naturally form strong capacity even though they possess the components of capacity with wealth resources and a security apparatus. Colombia's early leaders and population initially choose to form a weak decentralized state. However, when confronted by an existential threat, national sentiments began to change in favor of stronger state control. How did Colombia devise policies and use resources to change its institutional mechanisms and enable society to form a stronger centralized nation? How was Colombia's government able to expand its capability while simultaneously fighting a multifaceted enemy in civil war? Answering these questions will show how a strategy that develops components of state capacity, while simultaneously building security capability, is a

---

[77]Harvey F. Kline, *State Building and Conflict Resolution in Colombia, 1986-1994* (Tuscaloosa: University of Alabama Press, 1999), 1-28, 194-204.

more effective strategy toward achieving government victory during civil war as opposed to disproportionately focusing resources on security capability as the prime mechanism for defeating an insurgency.

As a colonial possession of Spain, the monarchy never established a bureaucratic mechanism to force Colombia's regional governors and landowners to comply with royal policies. Colombia's mountains, rivers, and jungle terrain favored a decentralized system where local rule and traditions were better suited to running the new nation. Private landowners financed and acted as the governing authority by making laws, paying police, and adjudicating disputes.[78] Government in Colombia formed around differing local interests that saw intrusion into regional affairs as domination and potentially detrimental to an area's economic prosperity. This had two effects: it solidified strong economic institutions that created a base for generating national wealth, but formed a subjective legal system whose enforcement relied on the capricious interests of differing local authorities. This dynamic remained compatible as long as different interests respected national trade laws when conducting commerce within Colombia, but each entity had the freedom for overseeing its internal affairs.

In 1886, Colombia's wealthy elites formed a national government[79] dominated by two parties--Liberal and Conservative.[80] Both parties were cautious not to create a strong military or national police force, fearful of one party dominating national security and were opposed to levying taxes on themselves. Therefore, the national government allowed regional landowners to raise local police forces necessary for serving a region's needs. Differing economic interests in Colombia also organized into powerful groups--like the National Federation of Coffee Growers

---

[78]Ibid., 9-11.

[79]Ibid., 12-13.

[80]James L. Zackrison, "La Violencia in Colombia: An Anomaly in Terrorism," *Conflict Quarterly*, (Fall 1989): 5.

and the National Association of Industrialists--gaining social prestige, while assuming governing responsibilities to collect "taxes" for investing into banking and infrastructure that benefited a particular industry.[81]

Forming a decentralized government, based-on localized interests, created a social identity based-on regional political interests as opposed to class or ethnicity.[82] Law became a subjective local matter not reflecting a standardized norm throughout the country. However, the nation's strong economic foundation later became critical in providing resources for expanding state capacity in times of crisis.[83] State capacity requires economic growth to provide resources for implementing policies, impartial rule of law to settle conflicts and create predictability, and professional bureaucrats to run governing institutions--like the military or social services. Colombia's decentralized governing mechanism began to consolidate the functions of these core capacities in the early twentieth century to form a stronger centralized state capability.

The rise of modernization in 1930s Colombia brought Liberal President Alfonso Lopez to expand state control by enlarging the electorate, enacting land reforms, supporting labor groups, instituting a secular government, and installing a "progressive income tax system."[84] State capacity increased as government created institutions to control economic, social, and territorial regions of the country--like customs houses, social services, and a larger military. However, these bureaucracies were not professional, but filled with partisans as a reward for their loyalty. Having wealth available enabled the Lopez government to change the state's direction to expand control over the population. However, Colombia still lacked critical enhancing mechanisms by not

---

[81]Kline, 12-14.

[82]Zackrison, 10.

[83]Kline, 13-14, 26-28.

[84]Zackrison, 5.

implementing an impartial legal system.[85] Therefore, the states' expansion conflicted with society's traditional governing relationship, and lacked popular support, since one group would benefit at the expense of another.[86]

Expanding state power without an impartial legal system to guide its actions, while excluding large segments of society, is an example of how poor leadership decisions can weaken state capacity. High stakes competition to control government led to a twenty-year civil war between Liberal and Conservative party interests called *La Violencia*. This war eventually cost 200,000 lives,[87] but eventually led Colombia towards an impartial legal and governing system. In 1952, as rural violence was at its height, a joint group of citizens requested the Colombian military to take control of the government and restore order.[88]

The military acted neutrally between the parties, implemented social relief, negotiated amnesty for various insurgents, and restructured the national police forces making them non-partisan. After six years of military governance, the Liberal and Conservative parties combined to form one power-sharing government called the National Front. The National Front represented both groups' interests and moved the state toward an impartial rule of law and governing system. This political agreement was overwhelmingly popular within Colombian society as it sought to share interests and end the nations' civil war. By 1965, criminal activity accounted for most of the remaining violence as Colombia's military had effectively isolated all remaining belligerents.[89]

The United States began its assistance to Colombia in 1961 during the last stages of its civil war. Most support focused on security enhancement as the Colombian military doubled from

---

[85]Kline, 13-14.

[86]Ibid.

[87]Zackrison, 5.

[88]Ibid., 6-7.

[89]Ibid., 15-16.

23,000 to 53,500 by 1966. America also directed aid towards counterinsurgent operations, intelligence collection, and civil-military programs.[90]

Colombian components of state capacity developed over time allowing the new National Front government to adjust its ability for controlling territory and citizen behavior. The nation's historically strong economic foundation, impartial rule of law, non-partisan police, and larger military, formed a more centralized capacity allowing leaders to shift policies in accordance with changes to the environment--internal and external. Although Colombian capability was still weak when compared to combined local interests, society's ability to generate wealth, combined with inclusive institutional mechanisms, and enabling societal conditions, shaped a foundation that allowed the state to regenerate its capacity for meeting future environmental challenges.

Lessons of Civil War and Growing State Capacity

One important lesson observed at this point in the case study is how political leadership, bureaucratic institutions, and popular will foster capacity through mutually supporting goals. Each component relies on the others for enhancing overall wealth and security. One sector choosing to dominate another weakens the overall process--such as interest based political class, unresponsive bureaucracy, or detached citizenry--thereby creating instability. Violence is the mechanism used by rebels to destroy wealth and halt administrative functions (public and private), causing the state to collapse through paralysis. Overtime citizens eventually change their views to garner peace.

In civil war, a state must first isolate violence from most economic sources to ensure resources are available for growing security. Expanding the economy becomes necessary to build a security force able to quell violence. To increase the economy requires implementing non-

---

[90]Kline, 15.

partial rule of law within secure areas, and making the state inclusive to the larger population. This necessitates resources for judges, investigators, and prison facilities to implement rules.[91] Demand for skilled professionals creates the need for social services--like education and healthcare--to produce a labor force for the economy, bureaucracy, and military. The increasing ability to expand these conditions after *La Violencia* eventually saved Colombia from its second period of major violence starting in 1984,[92] leading to a strong state enabling government victory during civil war.

Expanding State Capacity and Civil War Victory

Creating the National Front satisfied most Colombians, however, gave no voice to various Marxist "splinter-groups" who refused to put aside their ideology. To continue their violence these groups formed insurgent organizations,[93] such as the National Liberation Army (ELN), Revolutionary Armed Forces of Colombia (FARC), and Movimiento-19, to oppose and eventually overthrow the government. These groups survived by resorting to criminal activity and receiving external support from the Soviet Union and Cuba.[94] The Colombian state could not eliminate these groups using amnesty or military action, and became overwhelmed by violence in the 1980s with the rise of the drug trade.

The drug trade greatly destabilized Colombia economically and socially by overwhelming its financial system with a vast influx of illegally procured US dollars and offering criminal opportunities to the country's poor. Violence once isolated to rural farms during *La*

---

[91]Republic of Colombia National Planning Department and Department of Justice and Security, 14-18.

[92]Kline, 24.

[93]Zackrison, 15-16.

[94]Kline, 17-19.

Violencia, now proliferated throughout Colombia's cities. Insurgent groups and drug lords targeted government politicians, judges, police, and any other individual opposing their efforts.[95]

The influx of drug money gave resources to insurgents and drug lords providing those elements a capacity to better arm themselves against the military or national police, thereby removing security that prevented Colombia's justice system and social administrators from properly functioning.[96] Citizens formed paramilitary defense groups in response to the governments' inability to provide protection of their interests--as was the previous tradition.[97]

It seemed Colombia was moving back toward its old decentralized system, making various regions vulnerable to insurgent control. However, the state's social and economic core remained intact and was able to defend against this new violence as political leaders redirected resources into the state's security sector.[98] The government added seven percent to military and police budgets using funds from social spending between 1980 and 1990, where the military received $65 million worth of equipment after august 1989.[99]

While implementing policies to maintain a baseline of capacity and security for state survival, political leaders would not achieve government victory unless they grew greater capacity capable of sustaining military force needed to end criminal and insurgent activities. In 1999, with United States assistance, Colombia implemented the "Plan for Peace, Prosperity, and a Stronger State,"--known as "Plan Colombia"--later revised in 2002 as the "Democratic Defense

---

[95]Ibid., 21-23, 27-29.

[96]Ibid., 204.

[97]Ibid., 195.

[98]Ibid., 26-28, 195.

[99]Ibid., 98-199.

and Security Policy" (DDSP) by President Alvaro Uribe Velez.[100] The policy's objective was to regain control over the nation's territory.[101]

Lieutenant Colonel Juan Correa in his monograph "Stability Operations and the Colombian Army: A Case for Implementation of New Doctrine" lists the DDSP's five methods for achieving the government's policy goal:

Enlarge the military to operate in all regions to gain control and provide humanitarian assistance

Protect the population to foster development

Eliminate the drug trade

Maintain a deterrent capability after bringing a region under control, then focus on external threats

Conduct operations within the rule of law.[102]

The security plan focused on ending violence throughout the country by targeting terrorist and criminal organizations, and removing illegal groups' sustainment by destroying drug crops. Colombia implemented the "Protection and Promotion of Human Rights Policy" (HR) as a framework for providing relief until other social agencies could return to assist in humanitarian efforts that set conditions for government redevelopment.[103]

The results of these two policies reflect growing state capacity as they increased security forces by 32 percent, and built police stations within all 1,099 municipal governing seats. The policies formed new units, improved training, and purchased better equipment--like helicopters,

---

[100]Republic of Colombia National Planning Department and Department of Justice and Security, 7.

[101]Republic of Colombia Ministry of National Defense, 9.

[102]Juan C. Correa, "Stability Operations and the Colombian Army: A Case for Implementation of New Doctrine" (Monograph, School of Advanced Military Studies, 2010), 10-11.

[103]Republic of Colombia National Planning Department and Department of Justice and Security, 8-9.

patrol boats, and intelligence assets--to employ forces into fortified or remote insurgent areas. Within four years (2002-2006), the military demobilized 37,000 insurgents and caused the FARC to change its "concentrated offensive" strategy into "dispersed activities." Attacks on villages dropped from 32 to four, and of 131 mayors who found it too dangerous to perform state duties, by the end of 2006 only four were unable to function.[104]

Restoring and maintaining security in previously violent areas renewed public confidence (popular will) and allowed institutions to reestablish themselves, thereby attracting private investment. Colombian gross domestic product (GDP) grew from 1.93 percent to 6.8 percent between 2002 and 2006--the highest rate in twenty-years. This growth provided larger tax revenues that could support new state investments in social and security programs, revealing how public and private organizational dynamics (enhancing mechanisms and social conditions) foster wealth that lead to greater resources for growing state capacity. The Colombian government calls this process the "Virtuous circle of security" (figure 4).

Colombia's reinvestment toward enabling social components caused the poverty rate to decrease 10 percent and its unemployment rate to fall by 55 percent, demonstrating how minimizing violence and controlling territory allow private and social bodies to expand, subsequently bring about greater state capacity.[105] These results prove how the dynamic relationship between leadership, central capacity, enhancing mechanisms, societal conditions, the military, and wealth creation, interact to increase a states' ability for designing and implementing policies that achieve victory during civil war.

The "Protection and Promotion of Human Rights Policy" (HR), supporting the DDSP, set additional conditions to move newly controlled regions away from humanitarian support toward

---

[104]Republic of Colombia Ministry of National Defense, 16-17.
[105]Ibid.

reconstruction projects. This sought to reintegrate municipalities back into the state's central capacities. As security forces implemented relief, the HR took steps to build society's capability through the *Alternative Development Programs* and *Family Forest Guards*, benefiting 77,400 families who previously grew illegal crops. This brought 330,000 hectares of land back into the legal economy producing: coffee, cacao, rubber, palm oil, and forestry products. The HR policy also increased health coverage by 14 percent, covering 31.7 million people, increased education availability from 82 percent to 91 percent, and provided subsidies to 700,000 families benefitting one million children.[106]

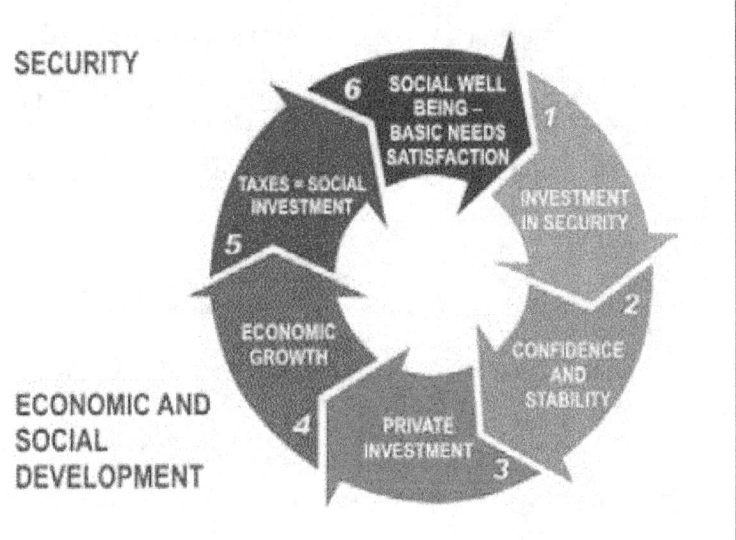

Figure 4. Virtuous Circle Graph
Source: Republic of Colombia Ministry of National Defense, *Policy for the Consolidation of Democratic Security* 17.

---

[106]Republic of Colombia National Planning Department and Department of Justice and Security, 9-10.

Colombia's success proves two points on how expanding state capacity supports government victory in civil war. First, it demonstrates the need to have a government ability to redirect resources for enlarging the military and providing relief within newly reclaimed territories. Expanding territory and supporting the populace garnered additional wealth and resources for continuing capacity building. Secondly, the states' ability to channel resources and take terrain from rebels conversely diminished the insurgents' resource base, and their capacity to carry-on civil war. Capturing and converting narcotics fields into legal crops deprived insurgent's financial means to sustain war, thus limiting their capability.

The DDSP, HR, and Plan Colombia policies also show interconnectivity between the three components of state capacity: central capacity, capacity-enhancing mechanisms, and enabling societal conditions. It is important to recognize that security achieved and humanitarian effort applied--while providing returns for state capacity--only set conditions allowing the government to solidify control. Reintegrating a territory back into the country creates the potential to expand state capacity.

Humanitarian programs, however, demonstrate that an area is not self-sufficient and risks collapse should the nation remove its support. Newly controlled areas rely on already existing resource capacity from stable regions for their survival and transition into a productive state entity. The state must take action to shift activities from humanitarian relief--which draws resources--toward making reclaimed territory a wealth producer that adds to overall state capability.

In 2007, the Colombian government transitioned the DDSP and HR to a new policy called the "Strategy for Strengthening Democracy and Promoting Social Development." This plan seeks to "consolidate" success by achieving added security for all citizens, and expanding development for the war on poverty.[107] The policy aims to reconstruct and reintegrate former rebel areas by using existing state capability for developing the base components of state capacity and wealth creation. This policy has six ways for implementing the program:

Continue the military war on terrorism and drug trafficking (central capacity)

Strengthen the justice system and promote human rights (enhancing mechanism and enabling societal conditions)

Open markets (enhancing mechanisms and wealth creation)

Create comprehensive social development (enabling societal conditions)

Provide attention to displaced persons (enhancing mechanisms and enabling societal conditions)

Continue disarmament, demobilization, and reintegration (central capacity)[108]

Military victory, previous policy success, and social strengthening, created popular support for state actions allowing Colombia's leaders the ability to increase taxes for garnering an additional $3.5 billion in the 2007-2010 budget. The government has planned $25.73 billion in resources to implement the new "Strategy for Strengthening Democracy and Promoting Social Development." Resources look to solidify the rule of law by resourcing officials to carryout investigations, adjudication, and punishment. Colombia will work to grow wealth by opening its markets and promoting investment equal to 25 percent of GDP. This will keep the economic growth rate at 3.1 percent and reduce unemployment to 8.6 percent of the labor force. The country will invest in building new roads, repairing existing roads, increasing river transport, and

---

[107]Ibid., 11.

[108]Ibid., 11-12.

expanding port facilities. The plan will also invest in rural agriculture, educational grants, and nutrition subsidies.[109]

By maintaining security in recently reclaimed provinces, and continuing offensive operations into other rebel-controlled areas, Colombia's government is simultaneously reintegrating its gains to expand capacity while continuing to work for military victory. By transitioning the DDSP and HR policies into the "Strategy for Strengthening Democracy and Promoting Social Development," works to move humanitarian recipients toward self-sufficiency by focusing resources on security, the rule of law, and wealth creation.[110]

The Colombian case study illustrates how a decentralized nation, with a purposefully weak capacity, was able to transition into a strong centralized state with capacity to stop violence and gain victory in civil war. Colombia transitioned because it possessed and maintained core elements of state capacity--recognized governing institutions, a capable society, private economic institutions, wealth creation, and a competent security apparatus. Having institutions and resources available, leaders were able to redirect policies, professionalize organizations, implement an impartial justice system, and expanded the military, as civil war conditions changed.

The success of the DDSP and HR policies followed-by the country's new plan to solidify control for expanding authority, demonstrate the linkages between capacity components and their variables. This study provides a holistic strategy example that creates sustainable capability allowing a nation time to develop for gaining victory in civil war.

The next case study reviews military and economic aid given to South Vietnam for building functions of state capacity. South Vietnam differs from early Colombian history because

---

[109]Ibid., 14-18.

[110]Ibid., 18-19.

as a kingdom the nation developed a centralized governing system with a strong capacity that enabled the kingdom's gradual southward expansion, adding the core capacities of modern administration and market economy as a French colony.[111] South Vietnam was a newly created country facing an internal insurgency and external threat from its Northern neighbor, which failed to build upon its historical institutions of state capacity--even while receiving massive U.S. assistance--resulting in government defeat. This study tests to find how political leadership, military strategy, and economic aid, worked to adversely dismantle South Vietnam's state capacity resulting in government defeat during civil war.

Case Study II: Deconstructing State Capacity in South Vietnam

This second study compares state capacity variables to the activities of the US and South Vietnamese governments' nation building efforts in South Vietnam to its counterinsurgency and conventional military strategies that resulted in North Vietnamese and Vietminh insurgent victory. *Viet-Nam: Politics and Public Administration*, by Nghiem-Dang, details Vietnam's state capability as an independent kingdom and French colony up through the nation's independence at the 1954 Geneva Accords. Nghiem-Dang provides an initial understanding of Vietnams' governing ability, allowing the reader to understand how U.S. intervention and the Saigon government dismantled capacity in South Vietnam. James M. Carter's *Inventing Vietnam: The United States and State Building, 1954-1968*, lists US activities and support given to South Vietnam, how South Vietnam used this aid, and how US efforts focused almost exclusively on a one-dimensional security building strategy.

Carter's work demonstrates how aid to South Vietnam sought to create a state capable of defending itself, yet lacked most institutional components of state capacity to enable the country

---

[111]Nghiem Dang, *Viet-Nam, Politics and Public Administration* (Honolulu: East-West Center Press, 1966), 2, 17, 30-35.

to function as a self-sustaining nation. *In Beating Goliath, Why Insurgencies Win*, Jeffrey Record informs this case study on how North Vietnam's capacity better managed its external support for defeating the South. Stronger North Vietnamese capacity was able to provide mechanisms for consolidating both nations into one self-functioning entity at the end of hostilities.

The United States Army in Vietnam, MACV, The Joint Command in the Years of Escalation, 1962-1967, by Graham A. Cosmas, provides a comparison to Record's book, citing how the allies' strategy changed within South Vietnam in response to conventional and non-conventional situations as they developed. Important to this monograph was the eventual creation of the Office of Civil Operations and Revolutionary Development Support (OCORDS) to oversee state building in South Vietnam. By applying the components defining state capacity, this book demonstrates that OCORDS was merely a better-organized action arm for providing humanitarian relief within a singularly focused security-building strategy similarly found in today's FM 3-07 and FM 3-24 doctrine.

It seems counterintuitive that South Vietnam's government would lose its capacity while receiving massive U.S. military and economic assistance to fight an insurgency and defend against a conventional war with North Vietnam. This study demonstrates how a strategy that predominantly focuses on building security capability may adversely affect components of state capacity, thereby making an ineffective strategy that unintentionally weakens government's ability to achieve victory during civil war.

Developing State Capacity in Vietnam

One thousand years of Chinese culture, the kingdom's southern expansion, and French colonial rule provided the basis for Vietnam's strong state capacity. After breaking from Chinese emperors in the tenth century, the Vietnamese Ly Dynasty (1009-1225) developed a centralized monarchal state who sectioned the country into twenty-four provinces ruled by princes and military commanders responsible to the emperor. Provinces later broke-down into districts and sub-districts, ending at the village level where mandarins administered each political entity.[112]

The mandarins were highly educated civil servants chosen by successfully passing periodic exams founded on Buddhism, Taoism, and Confucianism. Each mandarin was required to take an annual loyalty oath, and implemented the monarch's policies through persuasion, experience, and personal example.[113] This governing system slightly changed during the 1600s with the addition of two hereditary princes ruling in place of the king, where a "communal decentralization" policy began replacing village mandarins with village headmen chosen by the local population.[114] The two princes ruling in place of the king established a historical precedence for sectioning Vietnam into two parts, as the Trinh Family ruled north of the 18th parallel and the Nguyen Family ruled the south. Each family reigned for roughly two hundred years until southern Vietnam fell under French control in 1874, followed by the north ten years later in 1884. Although two families ruled Vietnam, this administrative change did not break the bond of Vietnamese unity, but served as a better way of governing a larger country.[115]

The creation of "headmen" at the village-communal level became the base of governing administration representing the states' core capacity. Popular will accepted this governing structure, as headmen were greatly respected individuals chosen by local people to carryout decisions based on "free-will." Nghiem-Dang calls this the "Principle of communal autonomy" where the commune became the primary entity for implementing decisions made by the central government (king and princes), or other local leaders.

---

[112]Ibid., 18, 22.

[113]Ibid., 1-3, 22-23.

[114]Ibid., 23.

[115]Ibid., 17, 23.

The ability for kings to collect taxes from its agrarian populace to resource state actions fell to a village council and its headmasters to gather. This illustrates how the interaction of capacity variables--core capacity, enhancing mechanisms and enabling societal conditions-- guided by accepted leadership, fostered a strong state capacity. The commune served as a collective taxpayer where the headman was able to meet any shortfalls by calling-on wealthier individuals to contribute extra resources to meet the difference. Taxes levied included a "head" tax and real estate tax.[116]

Using the "Capacity as a Dynamic Relationship Model" (figure 1) to analyze the Vietnamese Kingdom finds Vietnam held a strong governing capacity to implement activities and raise revenue by organizing the nation into provincial, district, village, and communal entities-- each administered by tested mandarins and chosen headmen, responsive to their feudal princes and the populace (core capacities). The kingdom based its laws (capacity enhancing mechanisms) on traditionally accepted Buddhist, Taoist, and Confucius teachings. These teachings guided kings and mandarins' decisions in forming and implementing plans of action. Society popularly supported imperial decrees and local decisions since officials needed to persuade citizens of their importance, and implement policies as best fit local circumstances.[117]

Wealth creation grew from agriculture and crafts, where the tax system and social-religious governing mechanisms allowed reinvestment for wealth creation. However, this did not specifically create greater resources for enabling societal conditions, but ensured a fed population and education availability for instructing future officials.[118]

---

[116]Ibid., 3, 5-7.

[117]Ibid., 1-3, 18, 22-23.

[118]Ibid., 5-7, 23, 34-35, 120.

This system allowed Vietnam's king the capacity to remain independent of China through most of the nations' history after breaking away in the tenth century, and provided the ability for the state to expand southward until making contact with French explorers seeking a trade route to China. When France gained Vietnam as a colony in 1884, colonial authorities worked to maintain the former kingdoms' governing structure, only changing areas necessary to carryout colonial policy for economic development.[119]

France introduced a market economy to Vietnam for creating industry and services that would expand wealth between the imperial power and colony. The French governor-general and colonists constructed roads, bridges, waterways, ports, and a postal system, while forming banks, professional organizations, and commercial investments.[120] However, French colonial governors also imposed land concessions confiscating thousands of acres of land for new settlers and those Vietnamese who assimilated to French custom. Villagers who lost their land became tenant farmers to colonial property owners.[121] Communal land held by village farmers fell to 2.5 percent of farmland by 1930, and the French made little effort at developing industry in Vietnam, only producing cement, ceramics, wood, leather, and rubber items, that employed roughly 150,000 people from a nation of thirty million.[122]

Seeking to maintain the order, colonial governor-generals kept the monarchs' centralized system to control Vietnam for economic gain, while further centralizing their power by controlling the colony's financial system to impose customs taxes and place monopolies on opium, salt, and alcohol. France used specialized services to direct and inspect activities--like

---

[119]Ibid., 2, 17, 30-32.

[120]Ibid., 31-35.

[121]James M. Carter, *Inventing Vietnam, The United States and State Building, 1954-1968* (Cambridge: Cambridge University Press, 2008), 38.

[122]Ibid., 37-40.

education; therefore, traditional Vietnamese governing and economic institutions began to interact with a new French system and modernizing economy.[123]

France placed colonial officers provincially to work with autonomous communal administrators. Specialized services--like land registration, health, and education--needed technical expertise to carryout, requiring state officials to interact more at the village level inspecting a local mandarin's work. Greater oversight led to a breakdown in the "autonomous commune" concept, heightening differences between French policy, actions, and placement exams--all based on a legal code--as opposed to the Vietnamese mandarin process, whose exams and governing methods were formed by Chinese studies and implemented through cultural beliefs, persuasion, example, and experience.[124] Colonial efforts at providing new public services and decentralize control did not bring the Vietnamese population to accept French rule, but continued to highlight differences in culture, thereby strengthening Vietnamese "national unity."[125]

Yet, by the mid-1930s, France had made Vietnam the worlds' second leading rice producer, making rice 65 percent of its exports, whereas industrial exports provided roughly six percent of Vietnams' output.[126] On the eve of World War II (WWII) 74 percent of Vietnam's economy consisted of agricultural and natural resource production, 13 percent formed manufacturing, and another 13 percent comprised public and private services.[127] The colony's infrastructure development reflected the need to facilitate wealth production where attempts at bettering societal conditions served as an afterthought--58 percent of imports to Vietnam went to

---

[123]Dang, 31-32, 34-35.

[124]Ibid., 2-7, 41, 120.

[125]Ibid., 32.

[126]Carter, 39.

[127]Dang, 34-35.

the colonial elite and the colony's defense apparatus. Vietnam had roughly 3,700 miles of road, and colonials controlled access to education allowing approximately 10 percent of the children to receive schooling.[128]

Over time, the interaction between colonial government and traditional Vietnamese institutional mechanisms for carrying-out policy became increasingly unpopular within Vietnamese society. However, as stated above, colonization-expanded Vietnam's state capacity by creating a semblance of industry, increasing agricultural production, introduced modern governance and a market economy, while building an infrastructure backbone for improving health, communication, and commerce.[129] Vietnam's agriculture served as the core of its wealth creation, as the nation continued to hold all components of a capable state capacity.

Vietnam's greatest need was to find a popular political regime acceptable to society that could reform its governing mechanisms--like land reform and educational access--thereby bettering social conditions for further expanding wealth creation, to better society and increase resources facilitating the states' ability for responding to national issues.[130]

Vietnam's war for independence with France affected core capacities after one-third of the nation's rail lines were destroyed; bridges, canals, and roads, became unserviceable making a large portion of South Vietnam inaccessible, thereby disrupting the rice trade (wealth creation), and providing a safe haven for Vietminh insurgents.[131] According to Graham A. Cosmas, in *MACV, the Joint Command in the Years of Escalation, 1962-1967*, this activity set conditions for the Vietnamese National Liberation Front (NLF) and the People's Revolutionary Party (PRP) of North Vietnam to later carryout insurgent activity into South Vietnam, by setting-up a "hierarchy

---

[128]Carter, 39-41.

[129]Dang, 2-7, 17-18, 31-35.

[130]Carter, 39-41.

[131]Ibid., 40-41.

of front and party committees" in the rural regions.[132] Additionally, most of Vietnam's industry and natural resources fell within the northern part of the country where the South traded its rice for Northern cement, coal, and rubber producing chemicals.[133]

France's defeat to Vietnamese insurgents in 1954 led to the signing of the Geneva Accords that formed two "regroupment zones north and south of the seventeenth parallel." The treaty required Vietnam to hold elections two years later in 1956 for deciding the nations' governing leaders who would unify the country into one entity.[134] Both North and South Vietnam inherited a historical legacy of centralized governance and self-rule under the Trinh and Nguyen families, possessed Buddhist and Confucius social-governing mechanisms, and enjoyed a productive agricultural-industrial wealth creating ability. Why was South Vietnam unable to harness this traditional capability to form a strong alternative to the communist system in the North? Why was vast U.S. military and economic aid unable to build upon these traditions to develop an independent South Vietnamese capacity capable of defending against its Northern neighbor and resulting in South Vietnamese government victory over Vietminh insurgents?

Dismantling State Capacity in South Vietnam

As cited in the literature review, there are five variables of state capacity: Core capacities (administration and military forces), enhancing mechanisms (rule of law), enabling societal conditions (health, education, and industry), popular acceptance of government, and wealth creation.[135] South Vietnam organized its provinces into districts, cantons, communes, and finally hamlets. The commune and hamlets served as the smallest administrative unit in South Vietnam,

---

[132]Cosmas, 71.

[133]Carter, 56.

[134]Ibid., 24.

[135]Kjaer, Hansen, and Thomsen, 21-25.

which formed forty-two provinces and two hundred and thirty-seven districts.[136] Its core wealth creator was rice production.[137]

The U.S. viewed the Geneva Accords' division of Vietnam within the context of the Cold War. U.S. policy sought to create a South Vietnam below the seventeenth parallel that was "an independent, non-communist state," thereby influencing American leaders to provide support to keep South Vietnam from merging with the communist North. This policy fit into the larger US strategy for strengthening South and Southeast Asia by forming an economic trade zone that included Japan.[138] However, Walter A. McDougall in *Promised Land, Crusader State, the American Encounter with the World since 1776*, categorized the U.S. plan for South Vietnam as "Global meliorism"--the socio-economic and politico-cultural expression of an American mission to make the world a better place. McDougall found U.S. policy in Vietnam became skewed by the "assumption that the U.S. can, should, and must reach-out" to assist other countries in attaining the American dream.[139]

In 1954, the U.S. mission in Vietnam created and implemented a political, economic, and military development plan that spent approximately $1.5 billion in six years between 1954 and 1960. The plan addressed all components of building state capacity, seeking to "instill" a governing president, recruit and train civil administrators, create a modern economy, form a new currency, build ports, hospitals, and schools, establish a transportation network, and finally, develop a national security force.[140]

---

[136]Dang, 120-123.

[137]Carter, 55-56.

[138]Ibid., 8-9, 23.

[139]Walter A. McDougall, *Promised Land, Crusader State, The American Encounter with the World Since 1776* (New York, NY: Houghton Mifflin Company, 1997), 173.

[140]Carter, 3-6, 10, 18.

However, state capacity building in South Vietnam became troubled at its inception when the Central Intelligence Agency's (CIA) Saigon Military Mission convinced U.S. officials to support anti-communist Ngo Dinh Diem over Emperor Boa Dai as South Vietnam's interim President. A national referendum held in October 1955 brought Diem to defeat Boa Dai after receiving a questionable 98.2 percent of the popular vote, making him South Vietnam's President. Realistically, Diem held a narrow base of support since the majority viewed him as a remnant of the former colonial system--a Catholic in a Buddhist nation. Therefore, Diem formed a closed non-inclusive government that denied political opponents access to decision making rather than forming a "United Front" government allowing Buddhists and other oppositions groups--like the Cao Dai, Hoa Hoa, and Bin Xuyen--representation.[141]

Excluding popular interests from government forced Diem to fill government agencies, police, and the military with political supporters who he trusted to carry out plans that the larger population would reject.[142] Diem's policies therefore needed to focus on controlling his opposition, while also defending against a North Vietnamese communist insurgency. Thus, laws and regulations (capacity enhancing mechanisms) arbitrarily favored supporters and interests of Diem's regime. The regime did not seek to invest in educational opportunities, business licensing, and healthcare access (capacity enabling societal conditions) to improve society, but instead used resources as favors to gain support for the regime. Therefore, the first eight years of South Vietnamese capacity building went toward securing the government against internal opposition and an externally supported communist insurgency.[143]

---

[141]Carter, 43-44, 59-63, 68-69.

[142]Cosmas, 82.

[143]Carter, 53-59, 60-70, 112, 145.

Diem's Presidential Ordinance Act of 1956 expanded the government's anti-communist campaign and justified arresting, jailing, and re-educating opponents of his government. Diem used the national army to control and defeat supporters of the Cao Dai, Hoa Hoa, and Bin Xuyen opposition groups. His success at controlling rival factions brought U.S. officials to view him as a strong leader and encouraged continuing support of his regime.[144]

The Michigan State University Vietnam Advisory Group served as the lead team for creating a governing apparatus in South Vietnam. Most of the team's time and resources went toward training and equipping a civil police force within South Vietnam. The U.S. Military Assistance Advisory Group (MAAG) assisted Diem in reorganizing the military and creating a paramilitary force to conduct counterinsurgency operations.[145]

The primary focus of building a strong security force organization, to protect the government from internal unpopularity and external aggression, shifted South Vietnam's economic development away from wealth creating industry capable of sustaining governing functions, into a temporary service economy dependent on continuous U.S. financial aid. American assistance between 1955 and 1959 paid for 85 percent of South Vietnam's imports to develop internal economic growth, pay government's operating costs, and expand consumer products within the market. However, of this aid 80 percent went toward South Vietnam's military budget. Officials spent South Vietnam's annual $166 million aid package on 45 percent transportation, 15 percent public administration, 9 percent industry and mining, 9 percent agriculture, 6 percent health, 5 percent education, 4 percent welfare, and 7 percent on various other projects.[146]

---

[144]Ibid., 62-63, 69-70.

[145]Ibid., 44, 66-69.

[146]Ibid., 75-77.

However, transportation and infrastructure development aid went toward facilitating military traffic, particularly the Saigon to Bien Hoa Road (core capacity) which cost more than "labor, community development, social welfare, health, housing, and education combined" (enabling societal conditions) during the 1954 to 1961 time period.[147] As U.S. troop levels expanded to 536,000 in 1968, U.S. military and economic aid vastly increased to $2 billion per year for supporting the military effort and expanding infrastructure to facilitate security operations.[148]

However, the great influx of American forces and assistance overwhelmed the national economy as inflation adversely affected the livelihood South Vietnams' population. Saigon's budget deficit grew 300 percent, its money supply expanded by 70 percent, increasing the cost of living in the country by 74 percent. By this time, government taxation accounted for only 7 percent of Gross National Product, demonstrating South Vietnam as completely dependent on U.S. financial aid for its resources.[149]

Increases in U.S. military and economic assistance did not contribute toward expanding South Vietnam's industry and core wealth creators, but adversely grew a service economy funded exclusively by U.S. aid supporting the defense of South Vietnam as its military expanded to 510,000 troops by 1964, and one million in 1973. During this same timeframe, the nation built less than twelve factories since 1954. Because South Vietnam was unable to sustain its own military expansion, and both governments took no action for developing self-sustaining industry, this service economy could not perpetuate itself once American aid ended. The nation's economy

---

[147]Ibid., 77.

[148]Ibid., 206-207, 218-219.

[149]Ibid., 174-176, 206-207, 218-219.

deteriorated to such a degree that by 1967, South Vietnam once the second leading exporter of rice needed to import 750,000 tons of the commodity to feed its people.[150]

The combination of an unpopular government and improperly targeted economic aid's adverse affects on South Vietnam's economy increasingly undermined the nation's capacity to defeat an insurgency[151] that appealed to "peasant aspirations" at the hamlet level,[152] and defend against conventional North Vietnamese forces. President Diem and the allies adopted a strategy called *Pacification*[153] that incorporated the ideas of Sir Robert G.K. Thompson's "Strategic Hamlet" strategy.[154]

The strategy called for military forces to "clear and hold" areas around the government's core region--Saigon--where police and administrators would follow-on to replace insurgent agents with pro-government officials. The final phase called for reeducating the population, implementing social and economic programs, and restoring order. To achieve this, the Strategic Hamlet program sought to group the rural populace into fortified communities allowing government forces to better control and protect remote populations from insurgent attacks.[155]

The underlying logic of this approach believed that by controlling the population, a government could gain popular support by providing social and economic benefits directly to the people, while denying resources to the insurgency.[156] Yet, as previously discussed, the vast majority of resources went toward supporting U.S. and South Vietnamese base infrastructure and

---

[150]Ibid., 212, 244-245.

[151]Ibid., 112.

[152]Cosmas, 72.

[153]Carter, 212-213.

[154]Cosmas, 76.

[155]Ibid., 75-76.

[156]Ibid., 76.

government administration. Due to political patronage, little spending went toward improving social conditions at the hamlet level. Therefore, Pacification adversely affected agriculture by moving people off the land or coaxed people toward more lucrative jobs in the service economy catering to U.S. forces.[157]

Additionally, the adversarial relationship between Diem's government and Vietnamese society was another factor hindering pacifications' success. The population rejected Diem's leadership on cultural and philosophical grounds; therefore, government services were unlikely to produce popular support for his regime. Additionally, the Presidential Ordinance of 1956 created legal mechanisms to justify controlling the population as opposed to defending society from a Communist insurgency. Hence, capacity's enhancing mechanism did not align to the military strategy.[158] Finally, South Vietnam's societal conditions did not provide officials with the technical expertise necessary to fortify villages and deliver planned services.[159]

By 1961, Communist insurgent organization and activities expanded throughout South Vietnam's rural regions.[160] Social tensions continued causing Diem to "crackdown" on Buddhist demonstrations, where after eight years the nation's Buddhists had developed a formidable political opposition to Diem's regime.[161] In November of 1963, political instability brought a coup toppling Diem's government, replacing it with a military panel called the Military Revolutionary Council (MRC) led by Duong Van Minh, later replaced by Nguyen Khanh. This coup did not rectify legitimacy problems within South Vietnam, but created more instability as six governmental leadership turnovers took place within two years between 1963 and 1965. South

---

[157]McDougall, 191.

[158]Carter, 60, 62-63, 68-70, 143-145, 156, 178.

[159]Cosmas, 87, 106, 140.

[160]Ibid., 71-72.

[161]Carter, 145.

Vietnam's core capacity to formulate and direct national policy became almost non-existent. The CIA assessed South Vietnam as "almost leaderless" and its governing mechanism "near paralysis" as it experienced military coups, ethnic-labor demonstrations, and riots.[162]

With the loss of government to provide leadership and direction, a weak societal capability, arbitrary regulations, and the loss of its wealth resources, South Vietnam had lost its capacity to function independently, thereby becoming reliant on U.S. and allied support to keep it a recognizable state entity. Graham A. Cosmas makes this point when discovering "the elimination of Diem did not fix South Vietnam's political, social, and institutional problems. The Governments fall only removed what administrative mechanisms the country had."[163]

South Vietnam now weakened by political and social turmoil, North Vietnam and its Vietminh insurgents began expanding the war southward against American and South Vietnamese forces, causing the U.S. to take-over the Pacification program in 1965. On 30 January 1968, a combined North Vietnamese conventional and South Vietnamese insurgent campaign took place throughout all of South Vietnam known as the Tet Offensive.[164]

Jeffery Record, in *Beating Goliath, Why Insurgencies Win*, notes that Vietminh and North Vietnamese People's Army of Vietnam (PAVN) Communist forces totaled roughly 300,000 active troops in South Vietnam during the Tet Offensive. These forces had the support of nearly 600,000 PAVN troops in North Vietnam, who received aid and assistance from the Soviet Union and China, creating a total force of approximately one million by 1973.[165] The Tet Offensive brought further destruction and havoc to South Vietnam creating one million new

---

[162]Ibid., 144-146, 151-154, 180.

[163]Cosmas, 106.

[164]Carter, 153-155, 241.

[165]Jeffrey Record, *Beating Goliath, Why Insurgencies Win* (Washington, DC: Potomac Books, Inc., 2009), 75.

refugees, freezing the economy, interdicting rice shipments along the Mekong River, and causing food prices to jump 300 percent. This added widespread looting and chaos to the list of social problems South Vietnam's government already lacked the capacity to address, and U.S. officials ignored, as American forces focused on defeating the Communist offensive.[166]

The U.S. government began to lose its political will for continuing the Vietnam campaign after the Tet Offensive. U.S. officials slowly began turning the war over to South Vietnam's government, and worked to revitalize the nation's capacity for defending itself against the North. However, over the next five years that the U.S. remained in country, officials continued to focus predominantly on security force development by doubling military aid from $1.2 billion to $3.3 billion between 1968 and 1973. This again expanded South Vietnams' military from 850,000 to one million troops while developing no internal capacity for sustaining such a large force, as U.S. economic and development aid would decrease from $651 million to $531 million during this same time-period.[167]

Eventually, all direct U.S. involvement in South Vietnam ended in 1973 after the signing of the Paris Peace Agreement.[168] The results of continuous war and South Vietnam's Pacification strategy changed the country's demographics from being an 85 percent rural agricultural nation, to a predominantly urban population. In 1974 roughly 65 percent of South Vietnam's people lived within a city. The refugee movement away from conflict zones destroyed the South's only source for wealth creation, and presented a humanitarian crisis to a government and bureaucracy unable to respond effectively[169] as the country's military was the primary focus of development since 1954. After the U.S. Congress ended all support to South Vietnam in 1975, the "politically and

---

[166]Carter, 241.

[167]Ibid., 244-245.

[168]Ibid., 244-246.

[169]Ibid., 206-212.

militarily weak client regime" had an economy unable to sustain government institutions, and suffered from internal political disunity, leading the country to fall to North Vietnamese conventional forces after two months of combat in 1975.[170]

Analysis and Conclusion

State capacity is the ability of a government to formulate and carryout policies, or plans of action, in response to internal and external environmental challenges. Three component categories interacting to determine capacity are central capacities (wealth creation, security force apparatus, administration), capacity enhancing mechanisms (rule of law, autonomous leaders, external agreements), and enabling societal conditions (education, health, industrial advancement). Military force and wealth creation are two critical variables within a nation's central capacities necessary for controlling a population and providing resources to implement government activities.[171]

Civil wars demonstrate "political instability" within a nation and work to destroy a state's wealth creation because the internal destructiveness prevents the population from privately reinvesting in their community. People fear risking personal wealth without having predictable regulations and the rule of law protecting their investments. As civil war conflict destroys wealth creation, it reduces tax collection, and the state loses resources necessary for maintaining control, thereby, diminishing state capacity.[172] Countries with popularly supported leaders involved in a civil war usually have stronger state capacity because government policies are more widely accepted and become enacted by national institutions.[173]

---

[170]Record, 82, 86-87.

[171]Kjaer, Hansen, and Thomsen, 10, 17-18, 20-24.

[172]Cardenas and Tuzemen, 2-5.

[173]Kjaer, Hansen, and Thomsen, 22-25.

The Colombia and South Vietnam case studies demonstrate how dynamic interaction between variables of state capacity, a nation's situational environment, and political leadership decisions, work to create strong state capability leading to government victory in civil war (Colombia), or adversely affected capacity's components resulting in weak capability and vulnerability (South Vietnam). Both Colombia and South Vietnam had high components of state capacity prior to their insurgencies. However, Colombia formed a broad-based popular government after its most bloody civil war--La Violencia--forming the National Front power-sharing government.[174] When an illegal drug trade expanded insurgent resources and intensified Colombia's civil war, the government was able to respond by implementing plans for protecting wealth-creating resources, while simultaneously expanding its security force capability.[175]

Colombia did this by working to isolate insurgent activity in contested areas near insurgent held territory, and better securing regions under government control. Once the government's military ability expanded--and was sustainable using internal resources--the state gained control over contested regions, while simultaneously striking into insurgent bases of support. Government assistance to reclaimed regions served as humanitarian aid and did not contribute to greater state capacity until established rule of law could sufficiently safeguard investments leading to wealth creation. After the Colombian government could reestablish the rule of law in reclaimed territories could its citizens invest in economic activity that later produced taxable resources for adding to the state's capacity.

This strategy reflects the approach advocated by Colonel Volckmann in FM 31-20 where a government divides its territory into three zones--government control, rebel control, and contested control--then works to isolate the insurgency from its bases of support. This allows the

_____

[174]Zackrison, 6-7, 15-16.

[175]Kline, 15, 26-28, 50, 198-199.

government time and space to build its capacity for conducting protracted offensive operations within contested regions and rebel controlled zones to destroy the insurgency.[176]

South Vietnam, however, had installed an unpopular governing leadership that led to continual friction in policy implementation, and required the nation's security forces to protect the government from both its population and a North Vietnamese supported insurgency. Rice production formed South Vietnam's primary engine for internal wealth creation, which fell under insurgent control or became the primary battleground for war as the state implemented its Pacification strategy.

The Pacification/Strategic Hamlet methodology led U.S. officials toward wholly directing aid at supporting military activities and expanding South Vietnam's security capability--like road, port, and base construction. U.S. officials neglected to develop aspects of South Vietnam that would later serve to support this growing security force. South Vietnam's economy shifted from agriculture to a service-based industry dependent on U.S. forces. Minimal resources went toward education or developing a new industrial economy for sustaining South Vietnams' growing urban population.[177] Resources spent to bring services into the hamlets served merely as humanitarian relief, as conflict and easy U.S. money dissuaded the populace from investing personal resources and effort at improving their rice production or opening new factories.

U.S. Military Assistance Command Vietnam (MACV) created the Office of Civil Operations and Revolutionary Development Support (OCORDS) as an organization for directing development in South Vietnam under a single unified command.[178] However, OCORDS simply became a more efficient organization at continuing a poor strategy for developing state capacity

---

[176]Birtle, 135-137.

[177]Carter, 75-77, 175, 206-212, 218-219, 244-245.

[178]Cosmas, 361-364.

in South Vietnam. By OCORDS not effectively addressing the political, economic, and social issues overwhelming South Vietnam's government, the country remained incapable of sustaining its growing military force, and meeting other demands within the rapidly changing situational environment.[179] South Vietnam's politically unstable government, unable to provide leadership in dealing with the nation's crises, caused state capacity to continually diminish until overwhelmed by its stronger neighbor.[180]

U.S. Counterinsurgency Doctrine and State Capacity Building in Afghanistan

According to the U.S. Senate Committee on Foreign Relations Report, "Evaluating U.S. Foreign Assistance to Afghanistan," nearly 77 percent of United States Agency for International Development (USAID) resources--totaling $1.65 billion--having been spent in Afghanistan's southern and eastern conflict zones between 2009 and 2010. Current projections for 2011 find resources to these areas will reach approximately 81 percent of money spent for "short-term stabilization programs instead of longer term development projects."[181] The World Bank's "2010 Afghanistan Economic Update" illustrates how this influx of aid into contested areas supporting the clear-hold-build approach has affected Afghanistan's development where "poverty mapping" throughout the country finds "most poverty-afflicted areas are not those in conflict."[182] The Senate Foreign Relations Committee report also discovered people living in Afghanistan's conflict zones are wealthier than people living in peaceful areas under government control.

---

[179]Ibid., 363-364.

[180]Carter, 144-145, 151-154, 180.

[181]U.S. Senate Committee on Foreign Relations, *Evaluating U.S. Foreign Assistance to Afghanistan* (Washington, D.C.: U.S. Government Printing Office, 2011), 8.

[182]Camil G. Osorio, Khalid Payenda, and T.G. Srinivasan, "Afghanistan Economic Update. Afghanistan Development Summary," *The World Bank* (2010), 11.

Poverty rates in "insurgency-plagued Helmand and Kandahar provinces are less than 30 percent," whereas poverty in the Central and Northern provinces of Afghanistan vary from "42 percent and 58 percent in Bamyan and Ghor to upwards of 58 percent in Balk province."[183]

Linking Afghanistan's capacity development program to the build phase of the clear-hold-build approach presents trends similar to those detailed within the South Vietnam case study. Afghanistan's 2010 Gross Domestic Product grew by 22.5 percent where economic growth expanded because of "private consumption … for goods and services from the increasing donor funding, the security economy, and an estimated external budget of around U.S. $4 billion." Communications is Afghanistan's largest growth sector at 45 percent, followed by finance at 27 percent, transportation 22 percent, agriculture 7 percent, retail 4 percent, construction 2 percent, and mining at 0.11 percent. Alarmingly similar to South Vietnam is Afghanistan's industry has contracted by 3 percent (-3 percent growth) creating a 12 percent decline in manufacturing.[184] This demonstrates that most of Afghanistan's resources come from outside assistance, thereby forming a dependent service economy incapable of sustaining itself--as occurred in South Vietnam. This currently makes Afghanistan's government vulnerable to collapse if foreign military assistance and development programs are withdrawn.

Foreign donor nations' resource and control 61 percent of Afghanistan's governing budget. Afghan officials control the remaining 39 percent of their expenditures, however, foreign aid accounts for 20 percent of this amount, meaning the international community resources a total 81 percent of Afghanistan's budget. However, what is positive of these numbers is that 19 percent of government funds are collected through domestic taxes and fees. This indicates that Afghanistan's core capacities and enhancing mechanisms are becoming capable of drawing

[183]U.S. Senate Committee on Foreign Relations, 11.

[184]Osorio, Payenda, and Srinivasan, 1-3.

resources internally from the populace. Yet, similar to South Vietnam, Afghanistan's security

sector accounts for one-third (33 percent) of the nations "internal budget" (money controlled by

the Afghan government), followed by education at 17 percent, agriculture at 13 percent, and other

private sector development investments forming roughly 4 percent of the internal budget.[185]

The U.S. Senate Foreign Relations Committee further reports that of the 61 percent

"external budget" not controlled by Afghan officials, money is potentially wasted by duplicating

donor resources, or implementing projects without plans for future sustainment--like the 16,000

Commander's Emergency Response Program (CERP) projects costing over $2 billion. The

Foreign Relations Committee finds that 97 percent of Afghanistan's Gross Domestic Product

comes from the international community's military and development activities. The report warns

that Afghanistan could undergo an economic depression after the projected departure of foreign

troops occurs in 2014.[186]

A More Effective Strategy for Building State Capacity to Achieve Government Victory during Civil War

Colonel Volckmann's approach for dividing a nation into zones of control enables a

government to build concurrently state capacity while isolating insurgent activity. Until a

government develops its national resources to a degree making the country self-sufficient can a

state pursue rebel forces continuously, as successfully demonstrated by the Colombian

government. Indicators of success found within the Colombia case study show a vast decrease in

national violence (security), effectively reinstating the rule of law, and increases to prosperity.

---

[185]Ibid., 7-8.

[186]U.S. Senate Committee on Foreign Relations, 2, 18-19.

Afghanistan has the possibility of attaining this success if foreign development aid shifts toward improving societal conditions (education, health, and infrastructure) and enhancing mechanisms (business friendly regulations, trade pacts) in peaceful regions of the country under government control. By simultaneously continuing humanitarian assistance, and denying key areas from insurgent forces in the South, will slowly grow the Afghan governments' ability to sustain a larger security force and provide responsive civil service institutions to meet demands of its continually changing environment.

Agriculture is currently Afghanistan's largest internal wealth producer outside of the aid driven service economy. The discovery of two mineral belts stretching from Heart to Badakshan in the north, and Kabul to Kandahar in the center of the nation hold an estimated $1 trillion resource reserve. Two mining projects currently under way to tap these resources at Aynak and Hajigak, may bring royalties to the government yielding between $208 million and $630 million per year after 2015--adding 1.1 percent to the nation's Gross Domestic Product. Depending on how Afghanistan regulates its mining industry and reinvests to foster "domestic activity" (enhancing mechanisms and societal conditions) will determine what it shall garner from these two projects.[187] While substantial, royalties from the two mining projects fall short of the $4 billion currently driving Afghanistan's development. This requires further expansion of enhancing mechanisms (external trade agreements, contract law) and improved societal conditions to grow the economic sector large enough for internally supporting the country's military and police efforts at defeating Taliban rebels.

Should this take place, overtime southern and eastern Afghanistan will need to decide if they want to join a more prosperous and inclusive center and north, or continue rebelling against a state with growing capacity that Taliban rebels can never overthrow.

---

[187]Osorio, Payenda, and Srinivasan, 1-3, 14-16.

Conclusion

Nations that focus efforts toward building security force capability without increasing state capacity are implementing an ineffective strategy for achieving government victory in civil war. To wage a prolonged civil war, nations must develop the ability to create wealth self-sufficiently for providing resources that allow adjustments to policies and plans as the situational environment changes. Countries without this capability who direct resources toward constructing a large military force, to defeat a rebel threat, may discover they lack the expertise and institutions necessary for reincorporating conquered territory back into their state as a productive entity.

Current US Army FM 3-07, *Stability Operations*, provides a useful doctrinal framework for developing state capability using tasks that direct resources toward bettering societal conditions, enhancing mechanisms, and overall central capacity. However, FM 3-24, *Counterinsurgency Operations*, presents a flawed methodology that inadvertently directs military and civilian leaders to focus development tasks within conflict areas where destructive violence prevents private investments from occurring. Resources directed toward conflict zones are simply humanitarian aid because they sustain a population, but do not create a resource surplus that improves society and adds toward expanding state capacity.

A more effective strategy for achieving government victory in civil war is to grow state capacity in peaceful regions under government control while simultaneously combating rebels and providing humanitarian aid in conflict zones. By isolating rebel violence within conflicted regions, leaders can apply aid in peaceful areas that reform enhancing mechanisms (regulations) and improve societal conditions (education), so investments can prosper without destructive violence, thereby allowing reinvestment to occur. These investments create a momentum that eventually produce the wealth necessary for a government to apply, and sustain, actions for defeating insurgents and reincorporating former conflict zones back into the nation's capacity.

Three indicators of a territory's moving from a dependent humanitarian-aid stage into a developmental stage are reduced levels of violence, state institutions administering the rule of law, and increasing levels of prosperity. A successfully reintegrated territory occurs when the region can function without government aid, and produces excess wealth for taxation, allowing political leaders resources to adjust policies in relation to changing world conditions. By growing state capacity in peaceful regions, a state builds resources to reclaim territory, sustain the territories population, and reintegrate the region back into the state's greater capacity mechanism. This removes resources from rebels, diminishing their capacity, resulting in a weakened threat. The states' continual capacity growth at the insurgents' expense eventually brings government victory in civil war.

BIBLIOGRAPHY

Besley, Timothy. "State Capacity and Development." Interview by Romesh Vaitilingam, *Vox Talks*. (June 2011).

Besley, Timothy, and Persson Torsten. "State Capacity, Conflict and Development." Monograph, St. Louis Econometric Society, 2008.

Birtle, Andrew J. *U.S. Army Counterinsurgency and Contingency Operations Doctrine, 1942-1976*. Washington, DC: United States Army Center of Military History, 2006.

Cardenas, Mauricio, and Didem Tuzemen. "Under-Investment in State Capacity: The Role of Inequality and Political Instability." *Global Economy and Development*, Washington, DC: Brookings Institution, 2010.

Cardenas, Mauricio, Marcela Eslava, and Santiago Ramirez. "External Wars, Internal Conflict and State Capacity: Panel Date Evidence." *Latin America Initiative*, Washington, DC: Brookings Institution, 2010.

Carter, James M. *Inventing Vietnam, The United States and State Building, 1954-1968*. Cambridge: Cambridge University Press, 2008.

Correa, Juan C. *Stability Operations and the Colombian Army: A Case for Implementation of New Doctrine*. Monograph, Fort Leavenworth, School of Advanced Military Studies, 2010.

Cosmas, Graham A. *United States Army in Vietnam, MACV, The Joint Command in the Years of Escalation, 1962-1967*. Washington, DC: Center of Military History, United States Army, 2006.

Daalder, Ivo H. "Decision to Intervene: How the War in Bosnia Ended." *Foreign Policy*, December 1998.

Dang, Nghiem. *Viet-Nam, Politics and Public Administration*. Honolulu: East-West Center Press, 1966.

de Rouen, Karl R., and David Sobek. "The Dynamics of Civil War Duration and Outcome." *Journal of Peace Research*, 2004: 303-320.

Dobbins, James, Seth G. Jones, Keith Crane, and Beth Cole DeGrasse. *The Beginner's Guide to Nation-Building*. Santa Monica: RAND Corporation, 2007.

Endres, Jurgen. *Shadow Globalization, Ethnic Conflicts and New Wars, A Political Economy of Intra-state War*. Edited by Dietrich Jung. London: Routledge, 2003.

Fienberg, Howard. "A Review of Making Democracy Work, a Book by Robert Putnam." *Howard Fienberg*. http://www.hfienberg.com/irtheory/putnam.html (accessed 8 August 2011).

Gallagher, Tom. *The Balkans in the New Millennium*. London: Routledge, 2005.

Garcia, Ed. *Internal Conflict and Governance*. Edited by Kumar Rupesinghe. New York: St. Martin's Press, 1992.

Gleditsch, Kristan Skrede, and Kyle Beardsley. "Nosy Neighbors, Third-party Actors in Central American Conflicts." *Journal of Conflict Resolution*, June 2004: 379-402.

Hendrix, Cullen S. "Measuring State Capacity: Theoretical and Empirical Implications for the Study of Civil Conflict." *Journal of Peace Research*, 2010: 273-285.

Hoffman, Frank G. "Hybrid vs. Compound War." *Armed Forces Journal*, October 2009: 1-2.

Johnson, Burke, and Larry Christensen. *Educational Research, Quantitative, Qualitative, and Mixed Approaches,* Second Edition. Boston: Pearson Education, Inc., 2004.

_____. *Education Research, Quantitative, Qualitative, and Mixed Approches Lecture 2.* University of South Alabama, October 6, 2006. http://www.southalabama.edu/coe/ bset/johnson/lectures/ (accessed September 2, 2011).

_____. *Educational Research, Quantitative, Qualitative, and Mixed Approaches Lecture 12.* University of South Alabama, October 6, 2006. http://www.southalabama.edu/coe/ bset/johnson/lectures/ (accessed September 2, 2011).

Khan, Adeel. "Pakistan in 2006, Safe Center, Dangerous Peripheries." *Asian Survey*, January/February 2007: 125-132.

Kjaer, Mette, Ole Hersted Hansen, and Jens Peter Frolund Thomsen. "Conceptualizing State Capacity." *Democracy, the State, and Administrative Reforms Research Report No. 6.* Aarhus: University of Aarhus, 2002.

Kline, Harvey F. *State Building and Conflict Resolution in Colombia, 1986-1994.* Tuscaloosa: University of Alabama Press, 1999.

Kocher, Matthew Adam. "State Capacity as a Conceptual Variable." *Yale Journal of International Affairs*, 2010: 137-145.

Kryzanek, Michael J. *Latin American Politics and Development.* Edited by Howard J. Wiarda and Harvey F. Kline. Boulder: Westview Press, 1990.

McDougall, Walter A. *Promised Land, Crusader State, The American Encounter with the World Since 1776.* New York, NY: Houghton Mifflin Company, 1997.

Osorio, Camil G., Khalid Payenda, and T.G. Srinivasan. "Afghanistan Economic Update." *Afghanistan Development Summary*, The World Bank, 2010.

Petraeus, David General. Interviewed by David Gregory. *Meet the Press,* 15 August 2010.

Poole, Walter S. *The Effort to Save Somalia.* Washington, DC: Government Printing Office, 2005.

Putnam, Robert D. *Making Democracy Work: Civic Traditions in Modern Italy.* Princeton: Princeton University Press, 1993.

Radu, Michael. *The New Insurgencies, Anticommunist Guerrillas in the Third World.* New Brunswick: Transaction Publishers, 1990.

Record, Jeffrey. *Beating Goliath, Why Insurgencies Win.* Washington, DC: Potomac Books, Inc., 2009.

Republic of Colombia, Ministry of National Defense. "Policy for the Consolidation of Democratic Security." 2007.

Republic of Colombia, National Planning Department, and Department of Justice and Security. "Colombia's Strategy for Strengthening Democracy and Promoting Social Development (2007-2013), Final Version." Colombian National Government, February 2007.

Sarkees, Meredith Reid, and Frank Wayman. *Resort to War: 1816-2007*. CQ Press, 2010.

Schmitter, Philippe C., Claudius Wagemann, and Anastassia Obydenkova. "Democratization and State Capacity." Research Thesis, San Domenico di Fiesole: European University Institute, 2005.

Schmitter, Philippe C., Claudius Wagemann, and Anastassia Obydenkova. "Democratization and State Capacity." Monograph, San Domenico di Fiesole: European University Institute, 2005.

Strazzari, Francesco. *Shadow Globalization, Ethnic Conflicts and New Wars, A Political Economy of Intra-state War*. Edited by Dietrich Jung. London: Routledge, 2003.

Toft, Monica Duffy. *Securing the Peace, The Durable Settlement of Civil Wars*. Princeton: Princeton University Press, 2010.

Torres, Ernesto C. "A Success Story of Philippine Counterinsurgency: A Study of Bohol." Master of Military Art and Science Thesis, Fort Leavenworth: U.S. Army Command and General Staff College, 2011.

US, Department of the Army. Field Manual (FM) 3-07. *Stability Operations*. Washington, DC: Government Printing Office, 2008.

_____. Field Manual (FM) 3-24, *Counterinsurgency*. Washington, DC: Government Printing Office, 2006.

US, Department of State. *Somalia*. September 26, 2011. http://www.state.gov/r/pa/ei/bgn/2863.htm (accessed September 29, 2011).

U.S. Senate. Committee on Foreign Relations. *Evaluating U.S. Foreign Assistance to Afghanistan*. Washington, D.C.: Government Printing Office, 2011.

Van Evera, Stephen. *Guide to Methods for Students of Political Science*. Ithaca: Cornell University Press, 1997.

Wright, Donald P. and Martin E. Dempsey. *A Different Kind of War, The U.S. Army in Operation Enduring Freedom, October 2001 - September 2005*. Fort Leavenworth: Combat Studies Institute Press, 2010.

Wuestner, Scott G. *Building Partner Capacity/Security Force Assistance: A New Structural Paradigm*. Carlisle: Strategic Studies Institute, 2009.

Zackrison, James L. "La Violencia in Colombia: An Anomaly in Terrorism." *Conflict Quarterly*, 1989: 5-18.

Zhang, Xiaoming. "China's Involvement in Laos During the Vietnam War, 1963-1975." *Journal of Military History*, October 2002: 1141-1166.

www.ingramcontent.com/pod-product-compliance
Lightning Source LLC
Chambersburg PA
CBHW082147290526
45794CB00008B/3191

* 9 7 8 1 4 7 9 1 9 4 1 9 3 *